SOLVE IT!

The Mindset and Tools of
Smart Problem Solvers

"I found Solve It! to be a practically useful, thought provoking and uplifting read which will be invaluable to experienced problem solvers and beginners alike. I love the way it combines techniques for getting the mind 'match fit' for tackling problems alongside practical and logical tools for solving perennial problems we all face once and for all!"

Jonathan Borrett, Head of Profession for Problem Solving,
Devon and Cornwall Police, Exeter, UK

"While many experts often focus on just the problem solving process, Dr. Sternad's important book does a great job of emphasizing the critical mindset needed to successfully engage in this process."

Edward C. Chang, Ph.D., Professor of Psychology and Social Work,
University of Michigan

"Solve It! is a highly accessible guide to problem-solving—whether at work or in life— that seamlessly integrates scientifically-rooted principles with practical guidelines and real-world vignettes making this well-rounded book accessible to and relevant for a variety of audiences, ranging from student to professional.

Jessica Mesmer-Magnus, Ph.D., SHRM-SCP, Professor & Chair, Department of Management,
Cameron School of Business, University of North Carolina Wilmington

"A great piece of work, which was much needed for spreading one of the most important skills in management!"

Roberto Quaglia, Ph.D., former consultant at McKinsey & Company
and Professor of Strategy and Management, ESCP Business School, Paris

SOLVE IT!

The Mindset and Tools of
Smart Problem Solvers

DIETMAR STERNAD

econcise
Concise books for smart learners

Paperback ISBN: 978-3-903386-03-7
ePub ISBN: 978-3-903386-04-4
Kindle ISBN: 978-3-903386-05-1

Copy editor: Harriet Power
Cover design: Farrukh_bala
Cover image and "lightbulb" image in the book: iStock.com/alphaspirit
Spiral-bound notebook image: iStock.com/Elena Rycova
Image on pp. 51 and 115: iStock.com/Shendart and iStock.com/fonikum

First published 2021 by **econcise publishing**
© 2021 econcise GmbH
Am Sonnengrund 14
A-9062 Moosburg (Austria)

www.econcise.com

Contents

Introduction

"It is not because things are difficult that we do not dare,
but because we do not dare that things are difficult."

Seneca the Younger

There is one skill that has the power to change the world. And it can change your life, too. This book will help you to build that skill—the skill of smart problem solving.

Problems—situations that are unsatisfactory and difficult to deal with—are a natural part of our lives. They are ubiquitous at work (solving problems is actually the main purpose of many jobs), but they also pervade our private lives. Just think about disagreements that you might have with a family member, financial difficulties, not finding enough time to adequately take care of your fitness, or a situation in which you are unable to decide about the right way forward.

In addition to the smaller and bigger problems that we all come across both at work and at home, there are the problems that our communities as well as humanity as a whole are facing: inequality, unemployment, pandemics, hunger, oceans full of plastics, climate change—to name just a few of the most salient ones.

Although human beings are natural problem solvers (that's what our brains are wired for), not everyone has developed the same level of problem-solving skills. There are those who tend to complain about everything and everyone, those who spend nights awake ruminating about a problem, and those who insist that 'someone' should do something about a problem (while at the same time implicitly making clear that they are not that 'someone'). Many people see problems without being able to solve them.

If you really want to change something for the better—whether it is in your work, your private life, your organization, your community, or for humanity as a whole—it is not enough to be a problem spotter. You need to become a smart problem solver instead.

As a smart problem solver, you will actively change things instead of just being a bystander:

- You will be able to overcome challenges in your work and life, and you will help others overcome their challenges, too.
- You will feel in control of your life.
- You will become more self-confident as you notice that you actually can get things done.
- You will be recognized and appreciated by others for your achievements and contributions.
- And by replacing lamentation with real improvements, you will make this world a little better.

The good news is that everyone can become a smart problem solver. You only need two things to make it happen: a *problem-solving mindset* and a *smart approach to problem solving*. This is exactly what this book is all about.

Part I of this book will help you to adopt a problem-solving mindset. You will meet some extraordinary smart problem solvers, and you will learn how they use the power of their mind to achieve what most others believed would be impossible.

With the right problem-solving mindset, you will be ready to make a positive impact in the world.

Part II is about rolling up your sleeves and actually getting your problems solved. The chapters in that part will guide you through the five main steps of a *systematic problem-solving process*:

1. **Clarify:** Define the problem, find better ways of looking at it, and understand the goals that you (and others) would like to achieve.
2. **Causes:** Learn more about the situation, identify possible root causes, and find out what really lies behind the problem.
3. **Create:** Be creative—with the help of smart tools and other people—and come up with potential solutions for the problem.

4. **Choose:** Weigh the pros and cons of your options and select the most promising one.

5. **Commit:** Translate your solution into concrete action and commit yourself and others to making it happen.[1]

Following these five steps will considerably increase your chances of finding a good solution.

The path to solving a problem is not always a straight one. As we will see later in this book, many problems are solved in iterations, which means that parts of the process may have to be repeated. You can also expect to meet obstacles and experience setbacks on the way. With this book as your guide, however, you can be confident that you will be able to find the right path in the end.

Not only will you be able to find clever solutions to your own problems and to the problems of your family, your organization, or your community—you will also develop one of skills that will be in highest demand in the future. Complex problem solving constantly ranks among the top skills in the World Economic Forum's *Future of Jobs* report.[2] Build your problem-solving muscle, and you will become more competitive in the workplace and enhance your overall ability to change things for the better.

During this journey, you will meet exceptional travel companions. Each chapter will introduce you to first-rate problem solvers. I hope that their stories will become an inspiration for your own problem-solving endeavors. In addition, you will gain a range of problem-solving tools that you can apply right away, as well as insights from the science of problem solving, which you can find in short summaries at the end of each chapter.

If you then—after reading the two main parts of this book—want to know more about how professional problem solvers work, check out the appendix ('Solve it like the pros') to get additional inspiration from scientists, doctors, designers, consultants, coaches, and expert negotiators—people who make a living from smart problem solving.

Are you ready for the journey? Then let's get started! Turn the page and start on your way to becoming a smart problem solver.

Problems are there to be solved!

··

ACCESS FREE BONUS MATERIALS

Solve your own problems with the help of the tools from this book:

- You can download **printable PDF versions of the problem-solving tools** from the book's companion website at *www.econcise.com/solve-it.*
- On the website, you can also download **free mindmaps** that provide a succinct, visual 'big picture' overview of the key concepts from this book, as well as **video links** related to selected topics in the books.
- If you are a lecturer who wants to use this book for teaching problem-solving skills to your students, we can also provide you with free, editable **Microsoft® PowerPoint slides** that you can use in your course (just send us an email to *lecturerservice@econcise.com* to get them).
- If you want to stay informed about current developments in the field and get more information about new books for smart leaders and learners, you are also welcome to subscribe to our newsletter at *www.econcise.com/newsletter*!

··

THE PROBLEM-SOLVING MINDSET

Smart problem solving is a combination of
smart thinking and smart acting.

It all starts with the right mindset.

Learn from the first part of this book
how smart problem solvers think (differently).

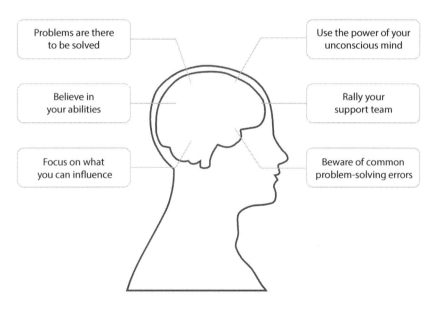

Figure 1 The problem-solving mindset

1

Problems are there to be solved

For every problem solved, there is someone who first believed that it could be solved.

Nelson Mandela believed that the problem of apartheid could be solved—and despite being faced with fierce resistance and spending decades of his life in prison, he succeeded. Apartheid was abolished, and Mandela build a new South Africa. When his party ANC finally won the elections in 1994, he said in his victory speech:

> *"We are rolling up our sleeves to begin tackling the problems our country faces."*[1]

These are the words of a smart problem solver.

The Wright brothers believed they could solve a problem that mankind had not been able to solve for tens of thousands of years: the problem of human flight. "For some years I have been afflicted with the belief that flight is possible to man," wrote Wilbur Wright in a letter to Octave Chanute, another aviation pioneer. "My disease has increased in severity and I feel that it will soon cost me an increased amount of money if not my life."[2]

The Wright brothers indeed spent a lot of money in following their belief. They had to overcome countless problems, tested hundreds of different designs, and failed in one trial flight after another. But eventually, they reached a breakthrough. They designed a practical flying machine that would take them up in the air—and into the history books.

The Wright brothers were smart problem solvers, too.

The story of Anne and Helen

Being a teacher myself, I am particularly fascinated by the story of another smart problem solver: Anne Sullivan.

Anne was in her early twenties when she became the teacher of six-year-old Helen Keller. After a severe illness during her infant years, Helen was left both deaf and blind. No-one could imagine how she would be able to succeed in school—no-one but Anne, who strongly believed that being deafblind was not a problem that should hold a person back from becoming an avid learner.

Yes, it was challenging. Anne first needed to make herself understood to the little girl, and Helen often refused to cooperate with her. Even in the rare occasions when she did cooperate, she was not really able to make sense of the finger spelling that Anne wanted to teach her. Helen became frustrated, and one tantrum followed another. But Anne did not give up. She recognized the problems, but she also believed that they could be overcome.

One day, Anne took Helen to a water pump. While the little girl had her hands in the water, Anne spelled w-a-t-e-r with her fingers. "I knew then that 'w-a-t-e-r' meant the wonderful cool something that was flowing over my hand," said Helen, later remembering that magic moment in her life. "That living word awakened my soul, gave it light, hope, joy, set it free! There were barriers still, it is true, but barriers that could in time be swept away."[3] In this magic moment, everything changed.

Things now had a name for Helen, and she became so eager to learn that she never stopped. Word by word, she began to understand the world. Anne also helped her to acquire reading skills in Braille, a special reading system where letters are identified by touching little bumps on a page. Eventually, Helen also learned how to talk.

With Anne's help, Helen succeeded in school and became the first deafblind person to earn a Bachelor of Arts degree at the prestigious Harvard-affiliated Radcliffe College.

Helen wrote a dozen books, made famous friends—including Charlie Chaplin, Mark Twain and Alexander Graham Bell—met with several US presidents, and became a vivid campaigner for the rights of people with disabilities, as well as for women's and labor rights.

"I do not pretend that I know the whole solution of the world's problems, but I am burdened with a Puritanical sense of obligation to set the world to rights,"[4] wrote Keller in one of her later works. She became a widely recognized role model as a problem solver, because she had an exceptionally smart role model herself—Anne Sullivan, the teacher who believed that problems are there to be solved.

The power of optimism

Problem solvers like Helen Keller, Anne Sullivan, the Wright brothers and Nelson Mandela are optimistic. Not in the sense of Voltaire, who described optimism as "the madness of maintaining that everything is right when it is wrong."[5] They do not run headfirst into the next wall just because they think that everything will always turn out well. They do, however, generally hold a positive attitude of confidence. They are confident that despite facing obstacles—which they expect—they will be able to change things for the better.

"Optimism is the faith that leads to achievement; nothing can be done without hope,"[6] wrote Helen Keller. The root of the word 'optimism' is the Latin *optimum*, which means 'best.' It is this quest for the best possible outcome in a certain situation—for finding a solution that really works—that is the driving force in the smart problem solver's mind.

The opposite of an optimistic problem-solving mindset is a pessimistic victim mindset. People with a victim mindset blame others for their situation. They are convinced that they have no control over events. Feeling powerless, they just accept their fate instead of taking action to change things for the better.

Many people tend to fall into the victim mindset, because it can actually be quite comfortable to be a victim. As a victim, you do not need to take any responsibility. You have a right to complain—and other people feel sorry for you. Feels good, right? Maybe—but it will definitely not solve your problems!

Who could have more reason to feel like a victim than the deafblind girl Helen Keller? But she made a decision. She would not be a victim. She would become an avid learner and a smart problem solver instead.

Taking control

As a smart problem solver, you don't say *"There's nothing I can do about it!"* Instead, you say *"I believe there must be a better way to move forward."*

You ask *"What can I do to change things for the better?"*—and you follow the example of one of the world's most renowned leadership experts, John C. Maxwell, who says, *"I am always looking for answers, I always believe that I can find them, and I'm always convinced that there is more than one solution to any problem."*[7]

With a problem-solving mindset, you do not blame others. You take control. You see yourself in the driver's seat, not just as a passenger—and you won't give up early when you face a challenge.

Yes, surely, you can expect a bumpy road ahead. Problem solving inherently entails challenges. It will not be easy—otherwise it would not need to be called 'a problem' in the first place.

Many people do not even try because they feel that the challenge is overwhelming. They think there's nothing they can do about it anyway. As a smart problem solver, you will acknowledge the existence of challenges, but you will not see them as unsurmountable obstacles. Instead, in every challenge, you will see an opportunity to grow.

"If we challenge ourselves to reach for something better, there is no problem we cannot solve," said former US president Barack Obama in his famous New Hampshire primary speech.[8] "Yes, we can! Yes, we can! Yes, we can!" he chanted. This is more than a political slogan. No matter your political leanings, it is also the battle cry of smart problem solvers:

"Yes, we can solve the problem—and we can change things for the better."

A little bit of science …
on the link between optimism and problem solving

- In a study among 211 college students, psychology professor Edward C. Chang observed that more optimistic 'high-hope' students had greater problem-solving abilities than their 'low-hope' peers. 'High-hope' students were also better able to cope with stressful situations during their studies.[9]
- Professor Gaye Williams of Deakin University (Australia) found that optimism supported elementary school students in their ability to collaboratively and creatively solve mathematical problems.[10] Isn't that great? Being more optimistic raises your chance of being good in math!
- A study by researchers from Michigan State University and the University of California (Davis) revealed a clear link between optimism and having a satisfying and happy romantic relationship. This was mainly explained by a higher degree of cooperative problem-solving abilities among partners with a more optimistic mindset.[11]

EXERCISE

Getting out of a victim mindset

It can be hard to shift your thinking if you've fallen into a victim mindset. But psychologists have developed an effective method to overcome the spiral of negative thoughts. This well-researched method is called cognitive behavioral therapy (CBT). It is often applied by professional psychotherapists in talk therapies. You can try out the main steps of a CBT process yourself:[12]

Step 1: *Describe the problem situation.* Write down what you are worried about. Once you have your problem written down in front of you, it is no longer locked inside your head, which means that it is easier to challenge.

Step 2: *Write down your thoughts and beliefs about the problem.* How do you feel about the problem? How do you typically react if you are faced with the problem situation? The purpose of this step is to make yourself more aware of your own thoughts and behavioral tendencies. Can you identify any negative or ineffective thinking patterns?

Step 3: *Dispute ineffective beliefs.* Take a second look at your thoughts and beliefs about the problem. Are they facts or opinions (and what's the evidence that they are really true)? Do your beliefs help or hinder you in reaching your goals?

Step 4: *Create a more effective outlook.* Think about a different way of interpreting the situation—one that turns negative thoughts and opinions about it into more realistic (and more positive) ones. What could you do to make the best out of it? What kind of beliefs and behaviors could help you to reach your goals? Which options do you have to overcome your challenges?

The main purpose of this process is to first increase your level of awareness of negative (or inaccurate) thinking, and then initiate a shift from a victim mindset to a problem-solving mindset.

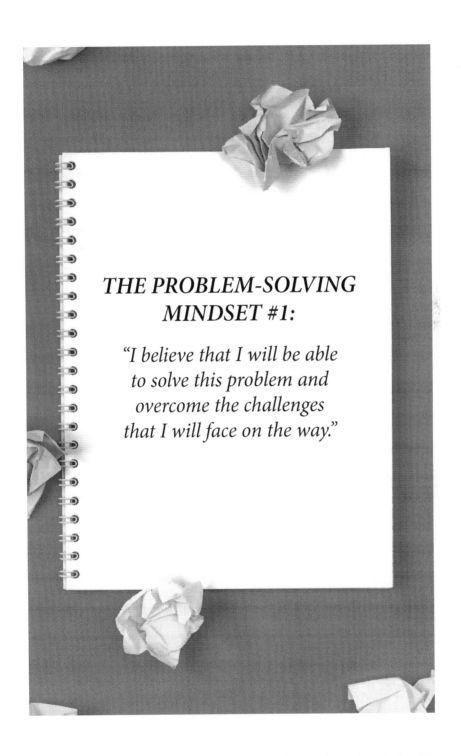

THE PROBLEM-SOLVING MINDSET #1:

"I believe that I will be able to solve this problem and overcome the challenges that I will face on the way."

2

Believe in your abilities

There is well-known story about a 15-year-old student at Laney High School. He loved basketball more than anything else in the world, and he desperately wanted to become part of the varsity team. Being convinced about his talent, he was sure that he would make it—until the day when the coach posted the team list without his name on it.

The boy was utterly devastated. "I went to my room and I closed the door and I cried," he remembered. He could not stop crying for a while and kept his door shut, as he did not want anyone to hear or see him.[1]

Sounds like a problem, right? Being on the team was all he wanted—and now he was officially told that he was just not good enough.

After what he saw as a big defeat, the boy could have given up playing basketball altogether. He could have blamed the coach. He could have resigned. But he decided to react differently. The boy continued to play in the junior varsity team and put in even more effort. He trained relentlessly. Whenever he became tired and was tempted to stop, he said, "I'd close my eyes and see that list in the locker room without my name on it, and that usually got me going again."[2]

Eventually, he succeeded. And not only did he make it into the varsity team. The boy—his name was Michael Jordan—became one of the most successful basketball players of all time.

A growth mindset

Michael Jordan is a prime example of having a *growth mindset*, which is another key ingredient of a problem-solving mindset. When you have a growth mindset, you believe that you can develop your abilities and skills through continued commitment and hard work. The opposite is a *fixed mindset*—the belief that if you are not good at something, you can never become better at it.[3]

People with a fixed mindset say *"Well, I am just not made for this."* Or they say *"I will never be able to solve such problems"* when they do not achieve what they want. If you have a growth mindset instead, you will not see failures as definitive failures, but only as temporary setbacks. You will embrace challenges as learning opportunities. And even if you cannot solve a problem yet (the little word 'yet' is particularly important here), you will be confident that you will be able to develop the skills that will help you to eventually find a solution.

With a problem-solving mindset, you will focus on moving forward when you face obstacles or challenges. As former rocket scientist and award-winning professor Ozan Varol explains, you will not see failure as a roadblock, but as "a portal to progress."[4]

With the right problem-solving mindset, every problem holds within it an opportunity to learn and grow.

Learning from failure

Speaking of rocket scientists, Varol also tells us the story of Elon Musk, the founder of the space exploration technology company SpaceX (besides a range of other companies that he also founded, including the electric car producer Tesla).[5]

In August 2008, SpaceX prepared the third launch of its first rocket Falcon 1. Musk had already invested a hundred million dollars into the project. The first two rocket launches had spectacularly failed. Actually, Musk was not having a good year at all. Shattered by the global financial crisis, Tesla stood at the brink of collapse. Musk had also recently gotten divorced. Falcon 1 was his lifeline.

At first sight, the third launch attempt started well. The rocket—carrying three satellites—perfectly lifted off the ground and soared into space. But then, at a critical point in the flight, with one part of the rocket detaching after running out of fuel and a second part ready to take over, disaster struck. Instead of falling away as planned, the first part fired again and crashed into the second one, resulting in a very rare rear-end collision in space. The rocket was lost and the mood of the team in the SpaceX factory "hung thick with despair," as one former SpaceX employee remembered.[6]

And Elon Musk? He came out of the control room and addressed his team. To their surprise and great relief, he informed them that he had already secured the financing of additional launches. He told them, as Shane Snow describes, that "they would learn what had happened tonight and they would use that knowledge to make a better rocket." This better rocket, he explained, would then be used for making even better ones, until one rocket would enable human beings to fly to Mars. Musk then closed his speech with the words "For my part, I will never give up. And I mean never."[7]

That's a growth mindset. The team soon found a way to solve the problem, and only five weeks later, the next Falcon 1 successfully took off from the launch pad. It became the first private spacecraft to orbit the earth—and just the first in a series of many successful launches (and a few more setbacks) to follow.

Smart problem solvers definitely do not want to fail. But they are clearly aware about the possibility of failing, and if they do, they learn and move forward.

A little bit of science ...
on the link between a growth mindset and problem solving

- The concepts of *growth mindset* and *fixed mindset* are based on the work of Stanford professor Carol Dweck, who has conducted extensive research on the positive effects of adopting a growth mindset. In one example, in a national study in the US, lower-achieving students were taught that they can actually develop their intellectual abilities. This short intervention led to a more positive approach to challenges and helped to improve the students' academic performance.[8]
- A growth mindset can also foster problem solving in the workplace. A study among employees of Thai manufacturing companies revealed that a learning orientation—the internal drive to develop and seek challenges that provide a learning opportunity—was positively linked with innovative problem-solving behavior.[9]
- It also works in the public sector! A study in a Norwegian government agency showed a strong link between the learning orientation of employees and their propensity to come up with creative ideas for solving problems in their work role.[10]

Shifting from a fixed mindset to a growth mindset

The research of Carol Dweck and her colleagues has shown that it is possible to shift from a fixed mindset to a growth mindset. Here is a process that you can follow to change your own mindset for growth:[11]

Step 1: *Listen to your inner voice.* If you are faced with a problem, can you hear yourself saying "I cannot do this," "I am not a good presenter," or "This is too difficult for me"? Then you have just identified your fixed mindset voice.

Step 2: *Use the power of "not yet."* These two short words have a strong impact on your thinking. If you tell yourself "I cannot do this yet" or "I haven't learnt how to be a good presenter yet," you open the possibility for being able to learn and grow.

Step 3: *Set yourself learning goals.* Which skills would you need to solve the problem, and which concrete steps could you take to learn these skills? Set yourself a small learning goal ("I'll watch a video of a highly successful keynote speaker, write down three things I notice about how she does it, and will try it out myself in the presentation I'm holding for my team next Monday"), and make one step forward. Reflect on what you have learned from the experience, and set the next learning goal.

Step 4: *Recognize progress.* Focus on improvements instead of on the final result. Praise yourself for daring to hold another small presentation or for writing down your learnings. The learning effort counts as much as the outcomes.

Note that shifting from a fixed mindset to a growth mindset involves both a tweak in your thinking ("not yet") and an active engagement in learning activities.

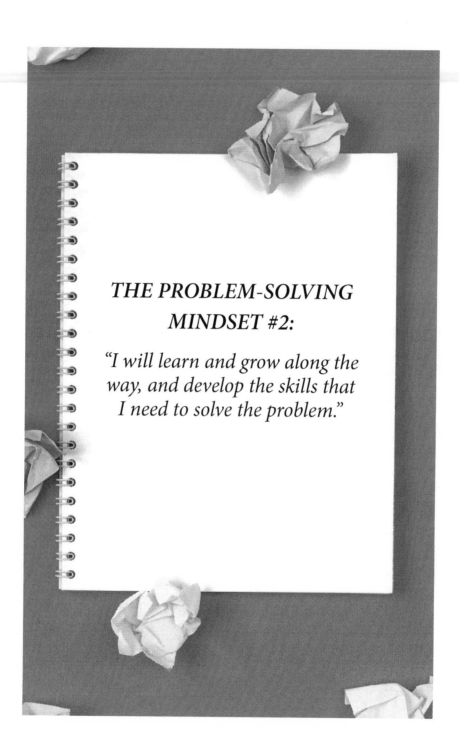

THE PROBLEM-SOLVING MINDSET #2:

"I will learn and grow along the way, and develop the skills that I need to solve the problem."

3

Focus on what you can influence

Marcus was 17 years old when his big problems began—and his problems were quite different from the ones that normal 17-year-olds face.

The Roman Emperor Hadrian had great plans for him. Hadrian did not have a son himself, so he decided to adopt Marcus—who had lost his father at the age of three—into the imperial family. He decided to develop him as a successor and heir to the throne. "What's the problem here?" you might ask. "Isn't it great to become a prince?"

Well, maybe not in this specific case. Reportedly, Marcus was actually quite sad when he heard the news of being chosen for the highest office of his times. Maybe he already knew what was lying ahead for him.

When Marcus Aurelius ascended the throne after some years of thorough preparation, the problems indeed started to flood in. Here is a considerably shortened list of the challenges he had to deal with (often at the same time):

- He had to fight fierce wars in many corners of the empire.
- His reign was overshadowed by a global pandemic, the Antonine Plague, in which millions of people lost their lives.
- A catastrophic flooding of the river Tiber left much of the city of Rome underwater.
- To make matters worse, his own men turned against him in an attempted coup led by one of his most trusted generals, Avidius Cassius.

In his private life, things were not going smoothly either. He suffered from recurring painful health problems, and eight of the thirteen children that he and his wife Faustina had died during their childhood.[1]

I think you will agree that by all measures, these are big problems. Anyone would need exceptional problem-solving skills to deal with all of them. Luckily, Marcus Aurelius possessed a very strong problem-solving mindset. As a smart problem solver, he found a clever way to deal with such an incredible amount of problems—simply by changing the way he thought about them.

The circle of concern

We all have a wide range of smaller and bigger things that bother us—at work (overload, an unfair boss, or colleagues who do not deliver what they promised), in our private life (problems with our spouse or children, or the feeling that we are not doing enough for our health), and in the wider community (seemingly incapable politicians, the widening gap between the rich and the poor, or climate change).

In some of these issues we become emotionally involved. The famous American educator and author Stephen Covey called these problems our 'circle of concern.'

People with a problem-solving mindset recognize that there are some things in their circle of concern that they cannot influence. They also understand that when they cannot really do anything about it, they do not have a reason to worry about it.

This resembles the basic tenets of the influential philosophical school of the Stoics, to which Marcus Aurelius felt strongly attracted:

- Know where you can change things and where you can't.
- Do not spend energy on what is outside of your control.
- Focus on where you can make a difference instead.

"To make the best of what is in our power, and take the rest as it occurs,"[2] is how the Stoic philosopher Epictetus, one of Marcus Aurelius's role models, succinctly summarizes the main idea of Stoic thinking.

Many people waste a lot of time and effort on things they can't change anyway. They complain about all the bad things out there in this world. But that's a problem-creating attitude, not a problem-solving attitude.

As a smart problem solver, you will only accept an issue as a problem if two basic conditions are fulfilled:

1. Importance: The issue is important for you.
2. Control: You can actually do something about it.

To clearly understand what this means for a smart problem solver, let us go through these two conditions one by one.

Importance

Marcus Aurelius was not only a Roman emperor, he was also a Stoic philosopher himself. He is the author of the famous *Meditations*, a journal that he wrote with the sole purpose of self-improvement. In that journal, he reminded himself not to forget that "care is to be bestowed on any enterprise only in proportion to its proper value. For if you keep this in mind you will not be disheartened from overconcern with things of less importance."[3]

In short: if something is not really important, then do not make a problem out of it!

Let us suppose you have a grumpy colleague who constantly complains about the various shortcomings of your organization's top management team. He thinks that this is 'a big problem.'

Is it really? With a problem-solving mindset, you will make the 'importance test' first. Are the alleged shortcomings of the top managers hindering you in reaching your most important work and life goals? In that case, you might consider them as a problem. Otherwise, they are just a circumstance that will not bother you any further.

Even when an issue passes the importance test, you will not yet be ready to accept it as a problem. It will first have to pass the 'control test', too.

Control

Can you actually *do* something that could change how the top management team thinks or acts? Probably not. Can you influence your colleague's innate tendency to be a constant complainer? Probably not either (unless you are a professional psychotherapist). So why worry?

In this particular case, the control test quickly revealed that this is *not your problem*. If you have no control over the issue, there's also no use spending energy on it. And there's no point in complaining about it either (unless it really makes you feel better).

As a smart problem solver, you will not allow everything in your circle of concern to become a problem. You will focus your energy on what Steven Covey called the 'circle of influence' instead—on those things where you can actually make a difference with your own actions.

For Marcus Aurelius, "planning your life, one action at the time" definitely makes sense, but only if you are well aware that "some external obstacles will be in the way." In that case, he suggests to accept the obstacles and then "good-temperedly alter your course of action," taking a new action that better fits your plan.[4] "The cucumber is bitter?" he asks. "Put it down. There are brambles in the path? Step to one side."[5] In short: accept external conditions that you cannot change as what they are—external conditions—and focus on what you can influence instead.

This doesn't mean that you shouldn't attempt to at least make a contribution to solving problems that might seem 'too big' for you to solve at first sight. Take climate change as an example. You can cut back on flying, eat less meat, and call on politicians in your country to take action. It might sound like a drop in the ocean, but many drops also make an ocean.

Sometimes, as we've seen above, a problem is simply too hard to influence and not worth fretting over, and taking a step back from it is the right thing to do. At other times, the problem is important enough that instead of thinking "this is outside of my control so I won't worry about it," a better attitude is "I'll focus on helping to solve this problem by tackling the bits I can influence."

Focus on inputs

What is definitely within our circle of influence are our own thoughts and behavior.

"If you suffer pain because of some external cause, what troubles you is not the thing but your decision about it," wrote Marcus Aurelius, "and this it is in your power to wipe out at once. But if what pains you is something in your own disposition, who prevents you from correcting your judgment?"[6]

Your own thoughts and your own actions—these are the inputs that you can influence. The outcomes—whether you will actually reach your goal or not—are determined by a combination of your own inputs and other factors over which you usually have less or no control.

Smart problem solvers therefore particularly work on their inputs—on their own attitude and actions.

As an entrepreneur, for example, you could set yourself a certain outcome goal. Let's say you wanted to achieve a 30 percent growth in revenues for your firm next year. That's fine. It is easy to set such a goal—but whether you will achieve it or not will depend not only on your own actions. It will also depend on a lot of other circumstances. Current market trends might play a role here, as well as the general economic situation or what your competitors are up to. These are all things that are out of your control.

What is within your circle of influence as an entrepreneur, however, is how you design your products, organize your sales, or motivate your team. This is where smart problem solvers will direct their efforts and energy—on where they can actually do something to change things for the better.

This does not mean that you should not have outcome goals. They are highly important for giving you meaning and direction. Most problems, however, will usually be solved on the input side. As a smart problem solver, you will therefore prefer to work on problems that are within your circle of influence.

Effective problem solving starts with working out which bits of the problem you can influence, and then focusing on improving the inputs to achieve better outcomes. That's what Marcus Aurelius did, and that's why he is still known—after almost 2,000 years—as one of the greatest emperors that Rome ever had.

Smart problem solvers follow his example, and they also follow the advice that Michael Phelps, the highest decorated Olympic champion of all time (with 23 Olympic gold medals), gave to all other Olympic athletes:

"Do what you can control, focus on what you can control."[7]

A little bit of science …
on the link between focusing on what you can influence and problem solving

- Psychologists distinguish between two types of goal orientation: *mastery orientation* and *performance orientation*. With a mastery orientation, you are focused on input-related goals (e.g. improving a certain skill, or doing something in the best possible way). When you have a performance orientation, you are mainly focused on reaching certain outcomes instead (e.g. getting better grades as a student, or winning a gold medal in the Olympic games as an athlete).
- In a study among 868 Indian managers, differences in the level of mastery orientation had a significant effect on job performance, while differences in performance goal orientation did not have any effect on performance at all.[8]
- Another study tested whether mastery orientation could actually be taught. One group of nursing students received a short-term educational intervention that helped them develop a stronger mastery orientation. These students were then found to be much more persistent in solving problems. Their colleagues, who did not receive the mastery orientation intervention, gave up much more easily when they were faced with a challenging task.[9]

Is it a problem that you should try to solve?

Use the following questions as a quick test to check whether you should try to solve a problem or not:

- *Is the problem really important for you?* Does it hinder you from achieving goals that you really care about? Is it worth spending your valuable time and energy on solving the problem?
- *Can you do something about it?* Could you take actions that at least contribute to solving the problem (even if they do not fully solve the problem yet)? Could you potentially influence others to take action to solve the problem?
- *Are you focusing on the bits of the problem that you can control?* Can you make a difference with your own attitude and actions? Are you directing your efforts toward the things you can influence?

Let a problem become your problem only when you can answer these questions with a "yes."

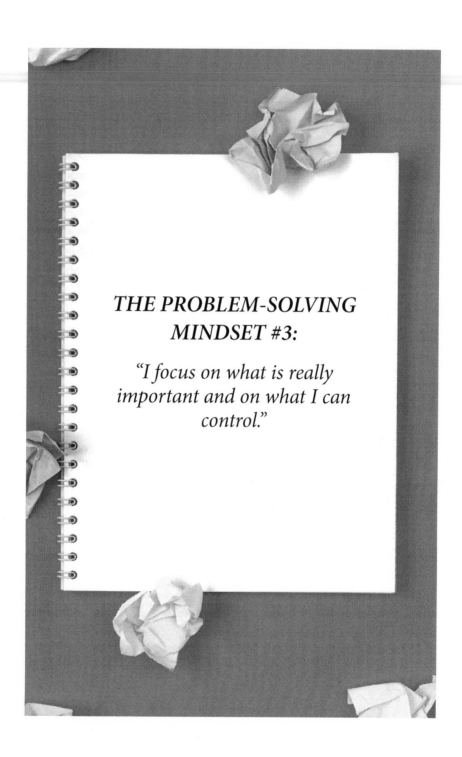

THE PROBLEM-SOLVING MINDSET #3:

"I focus on what is really important and on what I can control."

4

Use the power of your unconscious mind

Different people have different problems. Mathematicians, for example, have long been fascinated by a problem that nobody was able to solve for centuries: the problem of twin primes.

You've likely heard about prime numbers—those that you can only divide either by 1 or by themselves. A lot of these numbers come in pairs that just differ by 2, such as 3 and 5, 5 and 7, or 11 and 13. Although computers have been able to calculate a lot of these prime twins, generations of mathematicians were unable to find out whether an infinite number of these twins exists or not.

I know, for many of us, this might not sound like a highly relevant problem. Specialists in the field, however, considered the twin prime conjecture problem as nothing short of the "mathematical holy grail."[1] Scores of mathematics professors from all over the world have struggled with the problem, all of them failing to find a solution—until Yitang Zhang came along.

Zhang had a hard time getting recognized as a professional mathematician at all. For a long time, he had to work in a Subway sandwich store and as an accountant before he was finally offered a lecturer's job at the University of New Hampshire. He was still virtually unknown in the scientific community until that memorable day in April 2012 when he sent a paper to a scientific journal—a paper in which he claimed to have solved the twin prime conjecture problem.

Without going in depth (and humbly admitting that I actually do not understand all the details), he proved that "there is some number N smaller than 70 million such that there are infinitely many pairs of primes that differ by N."[2] This might not sound too grand for non-mathematicians, but the experts were flabbergasted. Zhang was invited to give a talk to mathematicians at Harvard University, and they confirmed that he had made one of the most important breakthroughs in the history of numbers theory.

Zhang had actually spent three years on the problem—three years without much progress. "I was so tired," he remembered. And then suddenly during a summer break, while he was taking a half-hour rest in the backyard of his friend's house in Colorado, the solution to the problem just appeared to him—virtually out of the blue. "I immediately realized that it would work," he said. And it did.[3]

Zhang's sudden, seemingly spontaneous intuition is evidence of the widely underestimated power of daydreaming.

Solve problems like Einstein and J. K. Rowling

Zhang is not alone. Albert Einstein found answers to complex problems when he was playing the violin. Churchill got new insights while he was painting. Physicist Werner Heisenberg came up with his uncertainty principle during a walk in the park in the middle of the night. And the story of a boy who attends a school of wizardry "came fully formed" into the mind of Joanne K. Rowling when she was forced to wait for a train to London that was delayed for four hours.[4]

These examples impressively illustrate the power of the unconscious mind.

Our conscious mind is a great tool for problem solving. It can help us acquire knowledge, structure problems, analyze ideas, and plan the right action steps for solving a problem.

But our brain has more to offer. It is much bigger than the small part in which our conscious mind resides. Smart problem solvers know that—and consciously make use of the unconscious part of their mind, too.

Are you getting stuck with a problem? Then follow the advice of the renowned psychologist Richard Nisbett: "Never fail to take advantage of the free labor of the unconscious mind."[5]

Just relax, do something else, and let your unconscious mind take over.

Eureka!

Even when you do not actively think about a problem, the neurons in your brain will continue to do their job. They will form associations and try to detect patterns. The unconscious mind is actually a real star in pattern detection. It is able to combine much more than you (consciously) think, including non-verbal cues that are difficult to express by the verbally oriented conscious mind.

When the unconscious part of your brain recognizes interesting patterns (or something that is clearly outside of a known pattern), it will send a message back to the conscious mind: "Hey, here's a point that's really interesting—could you maybe take a look at it?" That's what some people call an 'aha effect' or a 'eureka moment.'

Consider Richard Nisbett's cocktail party example. Imagine that you are in a nicely decorated room together with 30 other people. There is loud lounge music, and everyone is talking at the same time. You can barely understand the person you are currently talking to, and you do not hear anything else. But then, all of a sudden, you hear that someone who is standing further away is mentioning your name. Your unconscious mind did the job for you! It heard your name and recognized that this could be something of importance. You will now be able to consciously pay attention to what the party guest has to say about you (my best guess is that he or she will praise your exceptional problem-solving skills …).[6]

This is not Harry Potter magic. It is just how our brain works. And that is why problem solvers strategically make use of their unconscious mind. They prime the subconscious part of their brain with a problem statement (or even better, with a good question), and then resort to daydreaming, sleeping, playing a musical instrument, or doing other things that are completely unrelated to the problem. They do not force it when they get stuck. They let their unconscious mind do its job instead.

I just tried this once more myself. I'd got stuck with finding a good opening for one of the chapters of this book. When I went to bed, I silently said to myself: *"Dear unconscious mind, I need some help. Could you please think of a story as an opener for this chapter? This is the main message that I want to get across ..."* Then I fell asleep. My unconscious mind started delving into my memory, made connections, and formed associations. I didn't notice anything about this while I was sleeping, of course. But one of the first things that came to my mind in the morning was a story that was a perfect fit as a chapter opener. Of course, I didn't forget to say thank you to my unconscious mind for another great job done. Just try it out—it really works!

"Even when it's idling, the brain is still active," explains Ozan Varol. "You often have to wait away from the problem—literally and metaphorically—for the answer to arrive."[7]

A little bit of science ...
on the importance of using your unconscious mind for problem solving

- An experiment conducted by researchers from the University of Hertfordshire's School of Psychology found that an incubation period—some time spent away from the problem on completely different tasks—can significantly improve creative problem-solving performance. The researchers attributed this effect to the role of 'unconscious work.'[8]
- Researchers from the universities of Beijing and California (Irvine) observed that college students who were better in solving creative problems reported significantly more mind wandering during the incubation stage of the problem-solving process than 'non-solvers.' They concluded that the results of their research "suggest that mind wandering may play an important role in solving insight problems."[9]
- In two studies, 98 professional writers and 87 physicists, respectively, reported on what they were thinking or doing when their "most creative idea of the day occured." One fifth of the participants reported that their best ideas were formed during mind wandering that was completely independent of the task. These ideas were then also "more likely to be associated with overcoming an impasse on a problem and to be experienced as 'aha' moments, compared with ideas generated while on task."[10]

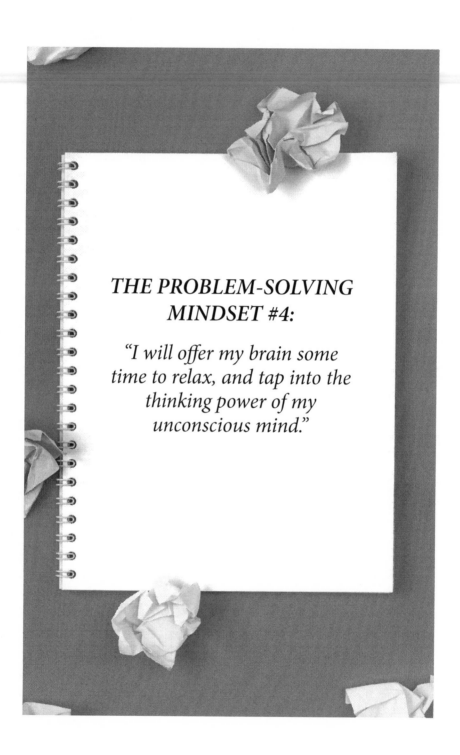

THE PROBLEM-SOLVING MINDSET #4:

"I will offer my brain some time to relax, and tap into the thinking power of my unconscious mind."

5

Rally your support team

During the final year of their master's studies, my graduate students work on a consulting project for local firms. The purpose of this team project is to help the firms enter a new foreign market. One of the key problems that students need to solve in this project is to develop an effective distribution strategy for the firm's products or services. To do so, they first need to understand how the distribution structures in the target market work.

The typical way in which students approach this task is to turn to the internet and start a Google search. They search for hours and hours, and often find it very difficult to come up with meaningful information, especially when they work in a very specific niche market (the market for ground water purification in Chile is one example from a recent student project).

There is usually one point in time when the students contact me again. "We have really done all we can," they tell me, "but we just can't find anything about the distribution structures in that particular market. All that we found is a report by a market research agency—but it is so expensive that we can't afford to buy it."

"Did you really do all that you can?" I ask them. "I understand that you did extensive desk research. But why don't you just get in touch with someone who knows the answer to your question?"

You would be surprised by how often I get an astonished look after posing this question. Suddenly, my students realize one of the best-kept secrets of smart problem solvers: you do not need to solve your problems alone!

One of the best ways to solve a problem is to ask others for help.

Problem solving is a team sport

For most problems, there is someone out there who has already solved the problem (with the twin primes conjecture problem being a notable exception)—or at least a similar one. Asking people who know more about the problem and its potential solutions for advice is one of the favorite shortcuts of smart problem solvers.

Once my students understand that, they change their strategy from searching for information themselves to identifying and contacting people who already know a lot about the issue. They might ask their home country's trade representatives in the target market for support, ask local distributors directly, or contact potential customers (e.g. water utility companies in Chile) and ask them which channels they use for purchasing their products.

My students are typically really surprised by how much relevant information they can get from talking to a local expert. In some cases, talking to someone with the right knowledge will enable them to solve their problem within a few minutes.

There are three questions that smart problem solvers always keep in the back of their minds during the problem-solving process:

- *"Who knows the most about this problem?"*—as they look for people who have domain-specific knowledge and experience with this problem.[1]
- *"Who has already successfully solved a similar problem?"*—these people could be a great source of ideas about how the problem could be solved and how to deal with challenges that could occur along the way.
- *"Whom could I include in my support team?"*

The last question differs from the other two. People who know the most about a problem or have solved a similar problem can provide invaluable information. People in your support team, however, will actively help you in your own problem-solving process.

Smart problem solvers know the value of viewing problem solving as a team sport. "Get other people involved as quickly as possible," is the advice of Thomas Wedell-Wedellsborg, a globally recognized expert on problem solving. He recommends working in groups of at least three when you want to solve a tricky problem, as one person can listen—and think—while the other two are talking.[2]

Share your problem with others, and you will get new perspectives, new insights, and new ideas. Use the power of multiplying brain capacity. A support team can help you to get a clearer picture of your problem, come up with more options, and choose the best way forward.

Choosing the right people

Speaking about making choices—choosing the *right* support team is key in this process. As a problem solver, you will prefer to rally people from outside of your own echo chamber. You will look for fresh perspectives, for outsiders who are "less emotionally attached to your preferred view of the problem (or solution),"[3] as Wedell-Wedellsborg suggests.

Above all, you will also want to see a problem-solving mindset in the people who you join forces with. Look for people who are positive and encouraging. Engage with those who see potential where others just see obstacles. Surround yourself with people who believe in you and your abilities—and stay away from those who put you down and drain your energy.

The members of your support team are your sparring partners in the problem-solving process. As Helen Keller said, "alone we can do so little; together we can do so much."[4] With strengths that complement your own, your support team can also play an important role in helping you to actually implement your solution. Think about which strengths and capabilities you will need to make a solution work, and make sure to include people with the right attitude and skills in your support team.

Even if you are a great problem-solving talent (of which I have no doubt), consider Michael Jordan's wise words: "Talent wins games, but teamwork and intelligence win championships."[5]

A little bit of science ...
on the role of teamwork for effective problem solving

- Researchers from the University of Illinois at Urbana-Champaign conducted an experiment in which individuals and groups of two, three, four or five people were asked to solve a problem in which they had to find out which ten numbers the researchers had randomly replaced with letters. The problem solvers could only find out more through proposing several equations to the researchers in letters (e.g. A + C = ?). They would then receive the answer in letters too (e.g. A + C = F). 760 people were included in the experiment. The results showed that groups of three, four and five people proposed more complex equations and needed fewer trials to solve their problems than individuals or groups of two. There was no difference in the results, however, between groups of three, four and five people. This led the researchers to conclude that "three-person groups are necessary and sufficient to perform better than the best individuals on highly intellective problems."[6]
- In an article called *Teams make you smarter*, researchers from the UK, Austria and the US reported a positive spillover effect of joint problem solving on subsequent individual performance. Reflecting on the findings of their study in which individuals and teams solved investment decision problems, the researchers said that they "can safely conclude that the experience of team decision making increases individual problem-solving skills."[7]
- Based on intensive field studies of work in professional service firms, researchers found evidence that collaborating with others can result in "a qualitative shift" in problem solving. Working with others can help people to better comprehend a problematic situation, generate more creative solutions, and gain new insights. These benefits are based on various forms of social interaction: seeking and giving help, reframing a problem with the help of different perspectives, and getting positive reinforcement from others.[8]

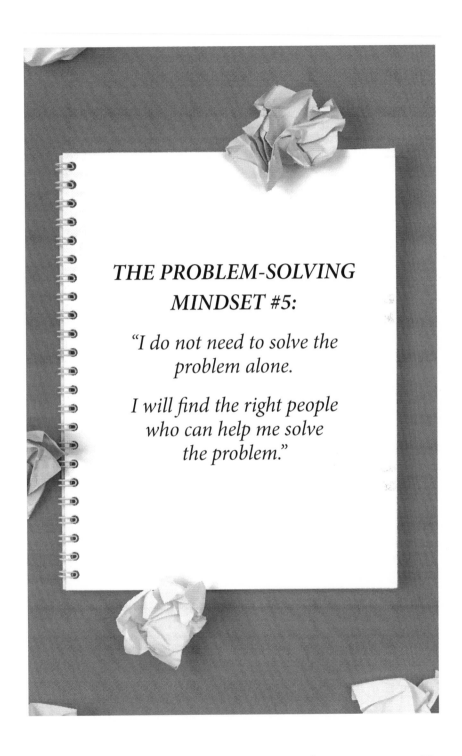

THE PROBLEM-SOLVING MINDSET #5:

"I do not need to solve the problem alone.

I will find the right people who can help me solve the problem."

6

Beware of common problem-solving errors

Here's a short summary of what we have already discussed: Smart problem solvers

1. believe that problems are there to be solved,
2. approach problems with a growth mindset,
3. focus on what is really important and what they can control,
4. use the power of their unconscious mind, and
5. ask others for help.

Following these five maxims will enable you to develop a powerful problem-solving mindset.

At the same time, smart problem solvers are aware that they must avoid falling into some dangerous thinking traps.

Our brains are incredible tools. They are nothing short of the best problem-solving machines on earth. Unfortunately, however, these machines are not always reliable. We are sometimes too quick to make assumptions and jump to conclusions, which is not always the best way to solve our problems.

Let us therefore take a look at three common thinking errors that smart problem solvers would definitely want to avoid.

Problem-solving error #1: Solving the wrong problem

It was 6:45am. As on so many mornings, the three kids were fighting again: Isabelle against Sophia, Sophia against Daniel, Daniel against Isabelle. Just like many other mornings, it was really hard to bear.

Their parents, Eleanor and Peter, had already tried everything they could think of to solve the problem. They had made their expectations clear, highlighted the importance of good relationships among siblings, taught them how to communicate with respect, and tried to instruct them how to channel their anger in a different way. They had mediated between the kids, rewarded them, punished them, talked with them, and begged them. But it was all in vain. The problem of the morning fights seemed impossible to solve.

The story about the never-ending morning quarrels between the kids was told by Peter Bregman, the father of the three kids, on the website of *Harvard Business Review*.[1] It is a great example of a problem-solving process that reached a dead end.

Everything tried, nothing worked. That's a certain sign that you are on the wrong track with your problem-solving approach. What you need is most probably not another solution—you need a new problem instead.

After countless failed attempts to solve the siblings fighting problem, the Bregmans gave up on their search for new solutions. Instead, they asked a completely different question:

"Is there another problem that we could solve?"

With this question in mind, Eleanor and Peter Bregman soon found out that there was indeed another problem—it was not a siblings fighting problem but a morning problem! The kids were just tired, and their blood sugar levels were low.

Finding a solution to this new problem was a no-brainer. Bring the kids to bed earlier, and give them a glass of orange juice when they wake up in the morning. Voilà, the morning fighting was dramatically reduced (everyone who like me has more than one child will know that it is almost impossible to prevent it completely).

This parenting problem is a great example of how our mind usually works. When we sense a problem, we immediately assume that we know what the problem is, and then we start looking for solutions right away.

Smart problem solvers think twice before they take a problem for granted. They know that the best solutions often lie in first making sure that you address the right problem before wasting your time with trying to solve a problem that actually cannot be solved.

This does not mean that you need to give up on your end goal. Of course, the parents in our story still wanted to have more peaceful family mornings. Taking your time to clearly define which problem to focus on, however, can be at least be as important as finding the right solution (we will discuss how to make sure that you're focusing on the right problem in Chapter 7).

Problem-solving error #2: Being too attached to pet ideas

Whether we are defining a problem or trying to find the right solutions, we are often prone to the next two thinking traps: selective thinking and assumptive thinking.

When we think selectively, we unfairly favor some ideas over others, such as certain assumptions that we hold about a problem situation or our favorite option for solving a problem.[2]

When we come across favorable evidence for our 'pet idea,' we warmly embrace it. In the case of unfavorable evidence, we discount it—or, even worse, we just ignore it. We all love it when our existing beliefs are confirmed, and we hate it when our assumptions are proved wrong.

Take the example of Blockbuster. It was an incredibly successful business that provided rental services for movies and video games. The company moved through a rapid international expansion. At its peak in 2004, it employed over 80,000 people in more than 9,000 stores worldwide. Despite evidence that mail order and video-on-demand services were on the rise, the company's management remained strongly attached to their pet idea that people would continue to physically borrow movies and games. When they slowly began to realize that customers were migrating to Netflix in scores, it was already too late. Blockbuster had to file for bankruptcy in 2010.

Being attached to pet ideas is closely linked to making wrong assumptions. The management of Blockbuster seemingly held the assumption that video rentals would always be made in physical stores.

Likewise, bank managers long assumed that their customers wanted personal service through bank branches (until internet banks took their customers away), Kodak's management assumed that photography meant film (until digital photography swept them away), and cab companies assumed they would always have a monopoly for transporting passengers around cities (until Uber came along). They all have one thing in common, and they all made the same mistake: treating assumptions as facts.

The folks from the internet banks, from Uber, and from all the other disruptive innovators chose a completely different path. Instead of taking existing industry assumptions for granted they decided to challenge them.

They asked themselves:

- What are the main assumptions (the 'invisible rules') in this industry?
- Why are things done in that way?
- What if these assumptions were not true?
- Is there a better way to solve the customer's problem?

"Many of our invisible rules were developed in response to problems that no longer exist,"[3] writes Ozan Varol. As a case in point, he refers to the QWERTY layout of typewriters. Modern computer keyboards are still designed with QWERTY as their first six letters. Here are the two problems that this layout solved:

1. It was designed to slow down typing speed to avoid mechanical key blockage.
2. Salespeople could use the letters in the first line to easily write the word typewriter for marketing purposes.[4]

Both problems obviously no longer exist. But as billions of people have already become accustomed with the existing 'solution,' any changes to it would become really costly.

As a smart problem solver, you will resist the urge to become overly attached to your assumptions and ideas. This does not mean that you are not allowed to hold a favorite idea in mind about what constitutes a problem and how it can be solved. We all prefer some ideas over others.

But it does mean you will always remain open to hearing and considering the facts—and when they speak loudly against your pet idea, you will be willing to let it go and adopt a new pet.

Problem-solving error #3: Misjudging other people

The third common problem-solving error is of particular importance in problem situations that involve other people. It is again linked to our assumptions—in this case the assumptions that we form about other people.

During my managerial career, I hired a lot of people. I remember interviewing one candidate for the job of a marketing director in a media company—let us call her Jessica here. Jessica performed exceptionally well in the job interview. She seemed to be keen-witted and highly knowledgeable in her field. She also connected really well with the three of us interviewing her. We were all fully convinced, so we decided to offer her the job right away.

It turned out to be a disastrous decision.

Soon after Jessica started to work as the new marketing director, we heard complaints about her from members of her team. She didn't treat them respectfully, they said, and made decisions that every marketing professional would regard as strange. The problems soon accumulated, as customers and partners started complaining about the "irritating behavior" of our marketing director. We knew that we had to act to avoid more damage, and negotiated a mutually agreed employment contract termination with Jessica.

In the end, this was not Jessica's fault—it was ours. We ran into a trap that psychologists call the *fundamental attribution error*. This is the assumption that the way in which people behave in one particular situation will give us a good indication about how they will behave in the future, too. When we fall into this trap, we fail to recognize that situational factors are highly important in determining how people behave. We believe that what we observe is a person's general disposition or personality, whereas it was really just a reaction to particular situational circumstances.

Jessica performed great in one particular situation—the job interview. But that was not the way she usually performed, especially not regarding her social skills. We could have given the fact that she had changed jobs quite frequently before more weight, or we could have asked former employers for a reference—but we didn't. We were blinded by the extremely positive experience in the interview situation.

As psychologist Richard Nisbett explains, the fundamental attribution error constantly gets us into trouble: "We trust people we ought not to, we avoid people who really are perfectly nice, we hire people who are not all that competent"—all because we do not consider the situational forces which can have an important impact on how people behave.[5]

Smart problem solvers understand that people behave differently in different situations. When they try to solve a problem that involves others (and a whole lot of problems do), they recognize that people can change when the situation or the environment changes.[6]

Solving the wrong problem, being too attached to your pet ideas, and misjudging other people—as a smart problem solver, you will be able to recognize these three common problem-solving traps—and you will by all means try to avoid falling into them.

A little bit of science …
on (avoiding) common problem-solving errors

- Roni Reiter-Palmon, a psychology professor at the University of Nebraska (Omaha), has conducted extensive research on what she calls *problem construction*: the process of finding and formulating the right problem before you attempt to solve it. Together with two colleagues, she observed a clear correlation between problem construction ability and the quality and originality of solutions.[7] These findings were confirmed when another team of researchers analyzed 40 studies in a meta-analysis in 2020. They also found a significant positive relationship between defining the right problem and finding more creative solutions.[8]

- Psychologists use the term *confirmation bias* for the tendency to favor information that supports the beliefs and ideas that a person already holds. Researchers have found ample evidence for the existence of that kind of bias. Even psychiatrists are not immune to it. A study conducted by a team of researchers from Germany, Austria, and the US found that psychiatrists who failed to seek evidence that might contradict their initial diagnosis of a patient made a wrong diagnosis in 70 percent of the cases.[9]

- Richard Nisbett, a psychology professor at the University of Michigan, conducted his own research and reviewed the research of others on the link between performance in job interviews and actual job performance. He reported correlations of less than 0.10 between predictions based on half-hour interviews and actual performance, no matter if it concerned medical students, army officers, or business people. "That's a pretty pathetic degree of prediction," explained Nisbett, "not much better than a coin toss."[10]

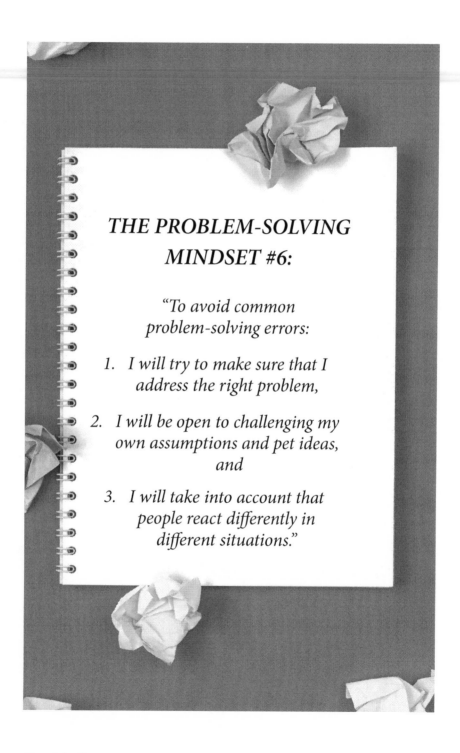

THE PROBLEM-SOLVING MINDSET #6:

"To avoid common problem-solving errors:

1. *I will try to make sure that I address the right problem,*

2. *I will be open to challenging my own assumptions and pet ideas, and*

3. *I will take into account that people react differently in different situations."*

THE PROBLEM-SOLVING MINDSET CHECKLIST

When you have a problem to solve, go through the following list and indicate whether or not you agree with the statements. Every "Yes" indicates that you already adopted a problem-solving mindset. The "No's" can help you to identify where you could still improve your problem-solving mindset.

Statement	Yes	No
I believe that I will be able to solve the problem.	○	○
I am confident that I will be able to overcome the challenges that will occur on the way.	○	○
I see the problem and potential challenges along the way as opportunities to learn and grow.	○	○
I believe in my ability to learn the skills that I need to solve this problem.	○	○
I do not waste time on issues that are not important.	○	○
During the problem-solving process, I focus on the things that I can influence (and do not worry about the things I cannot control).	○	○
I give my brain enough time to relax (e.g. in the form of sleep or daydreaming) to let my unconscious mind help me with my problem-solving task.	○	○
I ask other people for advice during the problem-solving process.	○	○
I am building (or have already built) a support team for solving the problem.	○	○
I have made sure that I am working on the right problem.	○	○
I know my main assumptions regarding the problem, and I am open to challenging them.	○	○
I am taking into account that people can behave differently in different situations.	○	○

Figure 2 The problem-solving mindset checklist

PART II

THE PROBLEM-SOLVING PROCESS

Smart problem solvers take a structured approach to problem solving.

They clarify the problem first, make a thorough diagnosis
of the causes, create a range of promising solutions,
choose the right one, and commit to taking action.

Learn more about the methods and tools that smart problems
solvers use during the problem-solving process
in this second part of this book.

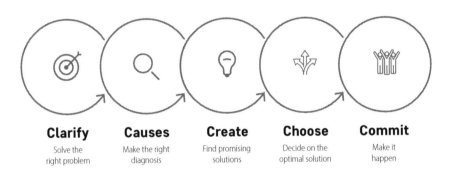

Clarify	**Causes**	**Create**	**Choose**	**Commit**
Solve the right problem	Make the right diagnosis	Find promising solutions	Decide on the optimal solution	Make it happen

Figure 3 The '5Cs' of the problem-solving process

7

Clarify: Solve the right problem

"The formulation of a problem is often more essential than its solution,"[1] said Albert Einstein, the epitome of a smart problem solver. He definitely knew what he was talking about.

As a smart problem solver, you will always want to clarify the problem first before jumping to conclusions. Finding the right answer to the wrong question won't help you much. Asking the right question is the first thing you will strive for instead.

Are you really trying to solve the right problem?

During the financial crisis of 2007–08, I was managing a book publishing company. It was one of a several dozen subsidiaries of an internationally active media corporation. The media industry was particularly hard hit by the crisis. Many business customers decided to radically cut their marketing spendings. Advertising revenues plummeted.

The senior managers of our media corporation reacted immediately. They instructed the managing directors of the subsidiaries to cut all cost positions by at least 20 percent for 2008—including labor costs. This was supposed to offset the loss in advertising income.

Due to the directive from the top management, all managing directors—including me—had a problem to solve. A 20 percent reduction in labor costs—that meant we had to decide who had to leave the company. There was no way to reduce costs by 20 percent without layoffs.

I'd always hated layoffs. It is one of the toughest decisions that managers need to take. But what could we do? It was our job to save the company, and we had a clear direction from our senior management team.

So we all got busy trying to find the right solution to this problem. Should we lay off the youngest employees first? Or those without a family to support? Those who only recently joined the company? Or maybe the underperformers? Every option had its pros and cons, and to be honest, the disadvantages prevailed in all of these 'solutions.'

As we were all desperately looking for the right solution for the layoff problem, one of our colleagues, the managing director of a national quality newspaper (another subsidiary of the media corporation), decided to question the problem statement instead. "Is there another way of looking at the problem than just having to lay off 20 percent of our staff?" he asked—and indeed, he found another way to formulate the problem statement. The question that he posed was simple and powerful at the same time: "Which other options do we have to offset the losses from the decreasing advertising revenues?"

As he discussed this new problem statement with his team, they soon came up with a solution. The newspaper had traditionally been published daily from Mondays to Saturdays. "Why don't we add a Sunday edition?" asked a smart member of the editorial team. "We could use our existing team and a few freelancers to produce it. And we could sell it separately in addition to the workday editions."

The team quickly embraced the idea. After all, it meant that there was a chance that no-one would lose their job. The new Sunday newspaper became an instant success. It reached much higher sales and circulation numbers than all the other editions. Out of a challenging situation, the newspaper company was able to complement its portfolio with a new star product.

With this simple act of challenging a problem statement—of rethinking what the real problem was—my colleague not only saved dozens of jobs. Together with his team, he also created a new winning product. He became a role model for all the other subsidiaries, where further jobs could be saved with more creative solutions for offsetting the lost advertising revenues.

Four steps to overcome the 'plunging-in bias'

The example of my colleague who was able to solve a problem through reformulating it illustrates the importance of clearly defining a problem before jumping into action (thus avoiding trying to solve the wrong problem, which is one of the most common problem-solving errors that we discussed in Chapter 6).

Smart problem solvers overcome the 'plunging-in bias'—that's what behavioral scientists call the tendency to start solving a problem before we even fully understand it.[2] They resist the temptation to immediately start with solutions, and instead make sure that they properly understand the problem.

The following four steps can help you to clarify the problem:

- **Step 1—Create a short written problem statement.** Writing it down forces you to think more precisely about what the real problem is. Writing fosters clarity. Deliberately formulating a problem statement will also help you avoid jumping to conclusions too early. It's a powerful habit of smart problem solvers, and easy to implement—just get pencil and paper (or a flipchart, if you are working in a group) and finish the sentence *"The problem is that ..."*[3]
- **Step 2—Clarify your goals.** Problem solving needs a clear direction. You need to know which goals you want to achieve, and what the ideal outcomes are. You will only be able to judge the quality of a solution if you know whether or not it will help you to achieve your goals. Smart problem solvers are realistic enough, however, to acknowledge that finding a 'perfect' solution that meets all their goals isn't always possible. That's why they will also think about what 'good enough' outcomes would look like.[4]
- **Step 3—Understand the goals of others.** Most problem situations involve other people. It is usually easier to resolve an issue if you know who else is involved, and what they want to achieve, too.

- **Step 4—Reframe the problem.** Once you have formulated the problem and identified the goals, take a step back and think once again. Could you think of a better way of formulating the problem?

Step 4 is particularly important—and probably one of the main factors that distinguishes smart problem solvers from those who tend to get frustrated because they are often reaching a dead end when they try to solve a problem.

"The problem is not always the problem"[5]—that's the advice of a former consultant of McKinsey & Company, a management consulting firm that receives incredibly high sums for helping to solve big problems in large organizations. Taking a step back and trying to find a different—and better—way of formulating a problem is also called 'reframing,' as you are looking at the problem through a different 'frame.'

The four steps of clarifying a problem are really crucial if you want to make sure that you are not wasting time working on the wrong problem. Let us therefore take a closer look at these four steps.

1. Create a short written problem statement

MIT professor Nelson Repenning and his colleagues called the ability of clearly articulating the problem to be solved "the most underrated skill in management."[6] A good problem statement, they argue:

1. focuses on an issue that really matters,
2. is connected to a specific goal you want to achieve,
3. includes a clear and measurable (at least in terms of 'better' or 'worse') articulation of the target, the current state, and the gap between them,
4. remains as 'neutral' as possible in terms of not unfairly favoring certain diagnoses or solutions, and
5. has the right scope (not to narrow, not too broad) that allows you to quickly tackle the problem.[7]

Take these two problem statements from our example above:

- *"How can we reduce our labor costs by 20 percent to offset the losses from the decreasing advertising revenues?"*

- *"Which options do we have to offset the losses from the decreasing advertising revenues?"*

Both focus on an issue that really matters (ensuring that the company remains profitable). Both are connected to a clear, measurable target and a gap (offsetting the loss of advertising business), and both have an adequate scope for finding actionable solutions.

The first problem statement, however, fails to comply with point four above. It is not neutral, as it already predetermines a certain solution. When the solution—in this case layoffs—is already 'baked into' the problem statement, you are missing out on the chance to find even better solutions.

Let's consider another example: "The problem is that I am too stressed in my work to find time for exercising in the evening." This problem statement describes an issue that matters to many people, and it is also connected to a specific goal (finding time to exercise). But is the target measurable? And is the problem statement really neutral? The diagnosis has already been made here—stress at work is the culprit. We are also limiting our options, as the problem statement assumes that exercising is only possible in the evening.

Let us reformulate the problem a bit: "The problem is to find time for at least two hours of exercising during the week." We can now clearly measure the outcome, and at the same time open up the space for new solutions. What about changing your Sunday morning routine from having a lie-in to going for a swim? Or could you maybe visit the gym during your lunch breaks in the week? With this solution, you could probably also reduce your stress levels at work.

Take your time to formulate a good problem statement. This is the first step to finding better solutions.

2. Clarify your goals

Whether a solution is 'better' or 'worse' depends on what you would actually like to achieve. Without knowing your goals, it is difficult to judge whether a potential solution will lead to the desired outcomes or not.

The senior management team in the example above set the following goals:

1. To keep the company profitable.
2. To make up for the lost advertising revenues.
3. To cut costs (including labor costs) by 20 percent.

My smart problem-solving colleague shared the first two goals, but realized that goal number 3 is actually not an end goal in itself, but just one particular option for reaching goals 1 and 2. And he had another goal in mind instead: to avoid layoffs. The new goal completely changed the direction of the problem-solving process.

As we can see from this example, our goals can widen or narrow our options space. Therefore, it makes sense to deliberately think about your goals—and ideally to also write them down—at the beginning of the problem-solving process.

But beware! If you have more than one goal, there might be trade-offs involved. A trade-off is a situation in which you cannot achieve all your goals at the same time, and you have to give up something you value to get something else that you also value. The two goals of avoiding layoffs and cutting labor costs are quite difficult to achieve at the same time, for example, so there's a trade-off involved here.

What can you do about trade-offs? First, simply set fewer goals! As long as you have only one main goal, there is no trade-off at all. The more goals you add, the more trade-offs are usually involved.

If you have different goals in mind, you could assess how important they are for you relative to one another. You could, for example, simply rate each of your goals on a scale of 0 = *unimportant* to 10 = *of utmost importance*. In the case of a trade-off, you would then prefer a solution that brings you closer to your more important (and higher-ranked) goals.

There is one more thing that you need to consider when setting your goals. Do you aspire for and will accept only the best possible outcome? Then you are a *maximizer*. The alternative is to accept a solution that is 'good enough.' In this case, you are a *satisficer*.

A maximizer would, for example, say "To reach my goal of two hours of exercise per week, I must exercise for at least for half an hour every Tuesday, Thursday, Saturday and Sunday." A satisficer's version is "To reach my goal of two hours of exercise per week, I'll start by exercising on at least two days, and give my best efforts to expand that to four days a week."

Research suggests that although maximizers often reach better outcomes when they solve a problem, they generally experience less satisfaction in life than satisficers.[8] The main reason probably lies in the fact that maximizers are in many cases not able to completely achieve all their goals, which makes them unhappy.

When setting your goals, you can also distinguish between ideal outcomes and 'good enough' outcomes. Again, this will open your solutions space. When you set a 'good enough' goal, you will still be happy even when you are not able to reach an ideal end state.

3. Understand the goals of others

You are not alone. Many—if not most—problems we are faced with involve other people too.

Consider our example from the media corporation I worked for again. The senior management had their goals. So did the managers of the different subsidiaries. But other parties were involved in this problem situation, too: customers, investors, and—with a particularly high interest in the problem—the employees. After all, they would be affected the most by a layoff decision, no matter whether they would be among those who had to leave the company, or among those who would have a lot more work afterwards.

As a smart problem solver, you will always try to consider the goals of others who have a stake in the problem situation (the 'stakeholders'). You can do so by asking the following three questions:

- Who else plays an important role in the problem situation?
- What are their most important goals?
- How might they see things differently?

You might, to return to our other example, also want to consider the interests of your family members when you try to find the best time for exercising during the week. How would they feel about your idea of going to the swimming pool on Sundays (maybe your spouse or kids would want to join you)? Or would they prefer you go to the gym during your lunch breaks, as that aligns with their goal of spending more time together at the weekend?

Taking the perspective of others into account early on can help you to find solutions which are beneficial or at least acceptable for all sides. It can also be an important first step for reframing the problem.

4. Reframe the problem

The change of the problem statement from reducing labor costs to identifying different ways to offset the advertising losses is a good example of the power of reframing. "By shifting the way you see the problem—that is, by reframing it—you can sometimes find radically better solutions,"[9] explains Thomas Wedell-Wedellsborg, who wrote a whole book about reframing a problem.

Investing a little time into thinking twice about whether you are really working on the right problem can help you save a lot of time and effort that you would spend on trying to solve the wrong problem.

In essence, reframing means digging deeper, with the clear aim of finding a better problem to solve.[10] In addition to perspective-taking ("What does the problem look like from the perspective of the other people involved?"), you could also use the following questions to reframe a problem:[11]

- Are we really pursuing the right goal? Might there be other/better goals to pursue?
- Can we reformulate a 'big problem' in a way that makes it easier for us to do something about it?
- What are the main assumptions behind our problem statement? What if these assumptions were not true?
- How would a complete outsider describe the problem?

Reframing is not a one-time activity. Experienced problem solvers use these techniques repeatedly. Throughout the problem-solving journey, they revisit the problem and ask: *Have we learned something new about the problem? Is this still the right problem to solve?*[12]

Restating your problem in different ways will raise your chance of finding a good solution.

And how do you know if your reframed problem statement is better than the original one? Just take a look at the five characteristics of a good problem statement again:

1. Does it focus on an issue that really matters?
2. Is it connected to a specific goal?
3. Does it include a clear and measurable target, the current state, and therefore the gap you're trying to bridge?
4. Is it neutral (without unfairly favoring certain diagnoses and solutions)?
5. Does it have the right scope that allows you to tackle the problem?[13]

Every good answer stems from a good question. Do not follow your first instinct to immediately find the right answer before being sure that you are trying to answer the right question!

A little bit of science ...

on the importance of clarifying your problem before looking for solutions

- In a much-cited study, Jacob Getzels and Mihaly Csikszentmihalyi found that the most creative arts students spent considerably more time in formulating a creative problem before coming up with a finished product (as a 'visible solution'). What's more, they also remained open to revisiting and revising their first problem definition during the later stages of the problem-solving process.[14]
- The importance of a thorough clarification of the problem for effective problem solving can already be observed at a very young age. Dutch researchers found a clear link between the quality of problem finding and the originality and completeness of ideas of primary students.[15] Another study revealed that 15- to 18-year-old students generated significantly more responses when they discovered and described a problem themselves than when they were just presented with a 'ready-made' problem.[16]
- Management professor Paul C. Nutt observed that half of the decisions in organizations fail. One main reason is that managers often define problems in a way that already points to a particular solution—which is often not the best one. Nutt suggests that managers should "open up the decision process to new possibilities" and "carry out an unrestricted search for solutions" instead of narrowly defining problems with an early bias toward a particular solution.[17]

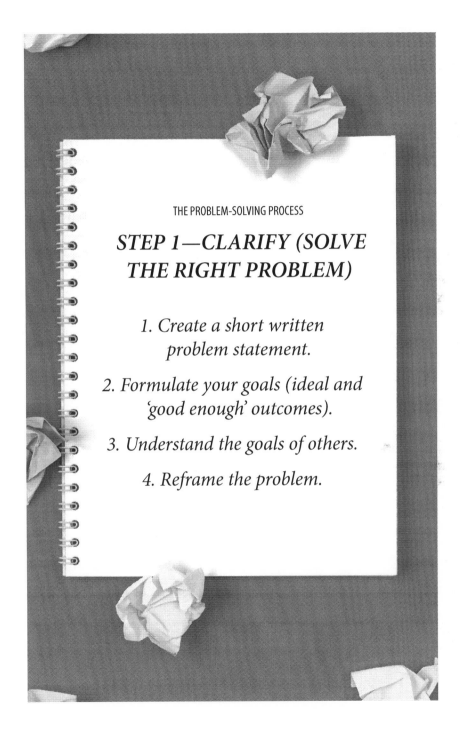

THE PROBLEM-SOLVING PROCESS

STEP 1—CLARIFY (SOLVE THE RIGHT PROBLEM)

1. Create a short written problem statement.

2. Formulate your goals (ideal and 'good enough' outcomes).

3. Understand the goals of others.

4. Reframe the problem.

PROBLEM-SOLVING TOOL

CLARIFY THE PROBLEM AND GOALS

Problem statement

The problem is that ...

My/our goals

Ideal outcomes

'Good enough' outcomes

Goals of others

Who? (stakeholder)

Their goal(s)

The problem reframed

The real problem is that ...

Figure 4 Clarify the problem and goals tool

8

Causes: Make the right diagnosis

Being a parent of two schoolkids myself, I was really shocked by a story that was reported by a German TV station. Following a wrong medical diagnosis, a 12-year-old girl almost died from suffocation.[1]

Celina had a very high fever and complained about a sore throat. As the symptoms did not subside, her parents decided to visit a local doctor's office. After an hour in the waiting room, the doctor's assistant called them into the consulting room. The doctor was out of office, so the assistant examined Celina's ear, nose and mouth and made two telephone calls with the doctor, who then made a remote diagnosis and prescribed antibiotics to combat a bacterial infection.

The following morning, in a dramatic turn of events, Celina had a strong rash and severe difficulties in breathing. An emergency ambulance brought her to a children's hospital. Her whole body looked like it was covered in burns.

The doctor on duty in the hospital quickly diagnosed glandular fever, a viral disease that is also widely known as the 'kissing disease,' named after one common way of catching it. Antibiotics are completely useless for viral diseases, and can even have the detrimental effect of causing a severe rash, as in Celina's case.

"The doctor's assistant could not provide the doctor with a suitable diagnosis, and got my daughter into this life-threatening situation," said Celina's father two months later. It was a close call, but with the right treatment in hospital, Celina survived, and her burns gradually disappeared.

Diagnosis before therapy

A therapy based on the wrong diagnosis is no therapy at all. Sometimes, as in Celina's case, it even makes things worse.

You cannot solve a problem well before you really understand its causes. That is why smart problem solvers spend enough time and energy on finding out what factors contribute to the problem before rushing to a solution.

"It is a capital mistake to theorize before one has data," said Sherlock Holmes in *A Scandal in Bohemia*. "Insensibly one begins to twist facts to suit theories, instead of theories to suit facts."[2]

Good doctors—and smart problem solvers in general—will first try to gather all the important facts before jumping to conclusions. They will only be confident in making a diagnosis and suggesting a treatment (or solution) when they have enough data to support their hypothesis about the root cause of a problem.

A good problem diagnosis usually involves the following steps:[3]

1. Gather data about the problem situation (the symptoms).
2. Identify all possible root causes.
3. Develop hypotheses about the most likely root causes and determine which analyses you need to make to test these hypotheses.
4. Only when the data tells you that you have with a high probability found the real root cause—start looking for solutions.

In the glandular fever case, the doctor and the doctor's assistant could have asked more questions to better understand the progression of the symptoms. They could have acknowledged that there are several possible root causes for the high fever and sore throat. Even if they considered a bacterial infection to be the most likely root cause, they could have treated their assumption as a hypothesis rather than as a fact.

To test their hypothesis about the type of infection, they could have run a blood test, checked the girl's tonsils, or felt whether her lymph nodes were swollen. It is highly likely that with such additional data, they would have noticed that their initial theory was wrong, and that glandular fever was the more likely root cause.

A lot of harm would have been prevented for Celina and her family if the doctor and the assistant had followed all the steps of a thorough diagnosis process and found the real root cause instead of just relying on their first gut feeling.

A good problem diagnosis is the best basis for finding a good solution. Let us therefore dig deeper and explore the four main steps of a good problem diagnosis in a bit more detail.

Gather data about the problem situation

"Data! Data! Data!" he cried, impatiently. "I can't make bricks without clay."[4]

—Sherlock Holmes in *The Adventure of the Copper Beeches*

We can only really understand a problem situation well if we have reliable data about it.

In most problem situations, we will be faced with both facts and opinions. "The girl has a high fever" is an objectively measurable fact. "I think that the fever is caused by a bacterial infection" is an opinion. Smart problem solvers make a clear distinction between facts and opinions. This does not mean that they wouldn't also take opinions into account. But they know the difference between "people say so" and reliable evidence.

Smart problem solvers are also aware of the possibility that seemingly objective facts may not always be 100 percent true. "There is nothing more deceptive than an obvious fact"[5]—that's a Sherlock Holmes advice again. What if the doctor's assistant looked at the wrong part of Celina's throat? What if the medical thermometer was broken? Admittedly, it's quite unlikely, but that does not mean it is impossible.

For really important facts, smart problem solvers will always check the source first. Where does the data come from? How has it been collected? Is the source reliable? Can it be trusted?

You might want to think twice when someone tells you that they have read about something "on the internet." Consider, for example, this text that was added to a Wikipedia article about the Cypriot football club AC Omonia:

> *"A small but loyal group of fans are lovingly called 'The Zany Ones'—they like to wear hats made from discarded shoes and have a song about a little potato."*

This is not a fact. It is complete nonsense. Nevertheless, a journalist from the *Daily Mirror* quoted this Wikipedia entry in his preview article for a match between AC Omonia and Manchester City.[6] The City fans then probably wondered where the Cypriots had left their discarded shoe hats during the game.

When checking the facts, smart problem solvers will also explore the context:

- Is there anything else that happened at the same time, or before and after the event?
- Are there other people involved in the problem?
- What were their actions, and what are their interests?
- What is my own role in causing the problem?

Understanding a problem situation means trying to find data about all the factors that could potentially affect the problem, including what is still missing. Seeing the bigger picture is the goal.

"Is there any point to which you would wish to draw my attention?" a Scotland Yard detective asked Sherlock Holmes in *The Silver Blaze*.

"To the curious incident of the dog in the nighttime," said Holmes.

"The dog did nothing in the nighttime," the detective replied.

"That was the curious incident," remarked Sherlock Holmes.[7]

Problem solvers gather information because they are curious to find out what happened and why it happened. On the other hand, they also avoid a situation called 'analysis paralysis.' When you gather more and more data and overanalyze an issue, you will also not be able to solve it, because you are no longer able to see the wood for the trees.

Only when you are confident that you have a good overview of the situation is it time to move on to the next step: identifying the root causes of the problem.

Identify all possible root causes

Some potential root causes for the problem may have already surfaced when you collected the facts about the problem.

Professional management consultancy firms (those who are paid a lot for solving problems) take this one step further. They often use what they call a 'logic tree' (sometimes also called an 'issue tree') as a graphical way of breaking a problem down into different causes.[8] The purpose of a logic tree is to see the complete picture of all potential root causes and avoid leaving an important root cause out.

Let us take a look at the example in Figure 5. It shows a very simple logic tree for the medical problem that we discussed earlier. The problem (high fever and a sore throat over several days) is stated on the left hand side of the tree. All possible root causes are then listed in a logically ordered way to the right.

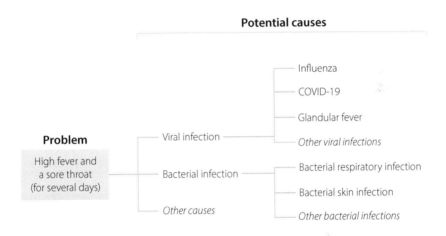

Figure 5 Example of a logic tree for identifying potential root causes

Working with such a tool can reduce the danger of just following the first instinct about what the root cause is (which might have potentially disastrous effects, as in Celine's glandular fever example).

For some problems, there are different ways of breaking them apart. If you have a problem in your relationship with your partner, for example, one way to start your logic tree could be to categorize potential causes under 'my own fault' and 'my partner's fault.' A slightly different way to break the same problem down into potential causes could be 'different expectations,' 'trust-related issues,' 'differences in priorities,' and 'communication issues.'

The way you structure the logic tree will have an effect on your next problem-solving steps. The 'my fault/your fault' structure will most probably lead to a more confrontational view of the problem situation. How happy do you think your partner will be if you confront them with a 'solution' that suggests they will have to change? The second way of breaking the problem down takes a different approach. It is based on the assumption that relationship problems are always two-sided, which means that the potential solution would also need to involve both partners.

In any case, using a logic tree should help you to get a more comprehensive overview of the potential root causes. It will also help you to avoid neglecting the possibility that there are other causes involved than the one that you intuitively favored.

A cleverly structured logic tree allows you to make use of the power of logic. As Sherlock Holmes said:

> "Crime is common. Logic is rare. Therefore it is upon the logic rather than upon the crime that you should dwell."[9]

Build and test hypotheses about the most likely root causes

Sherlock Holmes loved to work with hypotheses. As a master problem solver, he was certainly aware of what researchers today call 'confirmation bias': the human tendency to overvalue information that confirms what we already believe.

We are very fast in forming our beliefs. "High fever for a long time? That's an unmistakable sign of a bacterial infection," the doctor in our example probably believed. Once we have fallen in love with our beliefs, they become more difficult to challenge, even when we come across contradictory evidence.

To avoid falling into the confirmation bias trap, smart problem solvers think in hypotheses. A hypothesis is a temporary explanation for something. It is based on some known facts, but does not yet make the assumption that the explanation is necessarily true.

Experienced problem solvers also call it a *working hypothesis* to emphasize that the explanation is still "work in progress."[10] Unlike in the case of an opinion (which you defend), you are not emotionally attached to a working hypothesis.[11]

The main purpose of setting up a working hypothesis is to provide you with the opportunity to test whether your idea is true or not. When you test a hypothesis, you will be open to all possible outcomes. You are happy when you can prove that your hypothesis is confirmed, but you are equally happy when you need to debunk the hypothesis because the data speaks a different language. At least you have learned something valuable about your problem situation.

After having gathered enough data about a problem situation and having logically thought about all potential root causes, a smart problem solver will set up hypotheses for the most likely root cause.

Working with hypotheses in this way saves time. You do not need to investigate all possible options at the same time (which in many cases isn't feasible anyway). Two or three hypotheses linked to the most likely root causes will provide you with a clearer focus, and you can investigate each one separately. Through creating more than one working hypothesis, you avoid prematurely falling in love with one explanation, which could potentially be a pretty bad one (one of the most common problem-solving errors that we discussed in Chapter 6).

In our fever and sore throat case, the doctor could have set up two hypotheses, for example:

- Hypothesis 1: The reason for the fever and sore throat is a bacterial infection.
- Hypothesis 2: The reason for the fever and sore throat is glandular fever.

The next step would then be to determine which analyses still need to be made for testing each hypothesis, and which data is needed to either confirm or falsify them.

In the case of hypothesis 1, the doctor might want to conduct a blood test or send a swab from the patient's throat to a laboratory for examination. An elevated number of white blood cells would speak in favor of this hypothesis.

In the case of hypothesis 2, the doctor would probably want to make different tests, such as a physical examination of the patient's tonsils or of potentially swollen lymph nodes. Antibody tests could also detect Epstein-Barr virus, a common root cause of glandular fever.[12]

With such tests, the real root cause would most probably have been detected. Even if both hypotheses were falsified, we would at least have gotten one step further in our problem-solving process, as we ruled out two potential root causes, which considerably narrows the search space for other root causes.

Learning to think in hypotheses, finding the right tests to confirm or falsify them, and being open to proving yourself wrong—that's the way to identify the real root cause.

When the data indicates that you have with a high probability found the real root cause, then—and only then—it's time to start the search for the right solution.

> *"Watson: 'You may be right.'*
> *Holmes: 'The probability lies in that direction.'"[13]*

—Sherlock Holmes in *The Hound of the Baskervilles*

•••

 A little bit of science …
on the importance of identifying the root cause of a problem

- A study that analyzed the reasons behind 583 diagnostic errors made by physicians found that 44% of errors happened in the testing phase, as, for example, laboratory results were either not ordered, not reported, or not followed up. Clinical assessment errors (32% of all cases), failure to consider the whole patient history (10%), and errors in the physical examination (10%) were the other more frequently reported categories of errors.[14] The results of this study emphasize the importance of gathering data and testing hypotheses for solving (medical) problems.

- A study among Korean detectives showed that both the quantity and quality of the hypotheses they generated in simulated investigative scenarios was much lower when they worked under time pressure. In other words, the likelihood that detectives will come up with the right idea for solving a criminal case increases when they spend more time formulating the right hypotheses.[15] (Sherlock Holmes would definitely agree, as he usually prefers to take some time to think before rushing to conclusions.)
- In an experimental study, participants were asked to act as packaging machine operators with the task of finding and solving a problem in an industrial manufacturing process. One group of participants was only provided with raw sensor data, a second group with one hypothesis about what the data meant, and the third group with three competing hypotheses. The data-only group was a lot more inefficient in finding the right solution to the problem. Those with only one hypothesis were slightly faster than the ones with three competing hypotheses, but only when the hypothesis was correct. If their hypothesis was incorrect, they were three times slower than those who only worked with pure sensor data. The researchers concluded that "overall, providing several possible interpretations seemed to be the best strategy."[16]
- Professors Jessica Mesmer-Magnus and Leslie DeChurch analyzed the results of 72 research studies and found that information sharing has a strong positive impact on the performance of teams.[17] The more data the team members made available to each other, the better they were able to collectively solve problems.

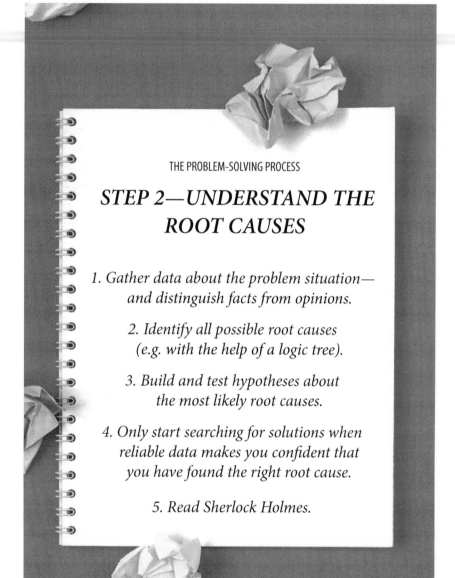

THE PROBLEM-SOLVING PROCESS

STEP 2—UNDERSTAND THE ROOT CAUSES

1. Gather data about the problem situation— and distinguish facts from opinions.

2. Identify all possible root causes (e.g. with the help of a logic tree).

3. Build and test hypotheses about the most likely root causes.

4. Only start searching for solutions when reliable data makes you confident that you have found the right root cause.

5. Read Sherlock Holmes.

UNDERSTAND THE (ROOT) CAUSES

The main facts about the problem

Facts	Source	Level of confidence in the source (1=low, 5=high)
		① ② ③ ④ ⑤
		① ② ③ ④ ⑤
		① ② ③ ④ ⑤

Potential root causes

Hypotheses about potential root causes	Analysis required to test hypothesis	Data source	Hypothesis confirmed?
			Ⓨ Ⓝ
			Ⓨ Ⓝ
			Ⓨ Ⓝ

Figure 6 Understand the (root) causes tool

9

Create: Find promising solutions

If you followed the steps in the previous two chapters, you should have already formed a good understanding of the problem. Now it's time to look for possible solutions and harness your creativity.

The main task in the 'Create' phase is to come up with several workable ideas for solving the problem. The more ideas you have, the higher the chance that you will be able to find a really good solution for your problem.

One of the secrets of creating smart solutions for difficult problems is to deliberately forget about limitations and constraints for a while. Don't worry, there will be still enough time to assess and judge ideas in the next phase of the problem-solving process ('Choose'). For now, there is only one task: generating a range of different creative ideas for how the problem could be solved.

Solving the puzzle

Here's an old story that I traced back to 1935 (although back then, the author acknowledged that it had been told before):[1]

A father was spending an evening alone with his six-year-old daughter. He wanted to read his evening newspaper, while his daughter constantly interrupted him. She was obviously quite bored, and wanted someone to play with (which reminds me of my own little daughter).

The father thought that he had found a great idea to keep her busy. There was a map of the world on one page of his newspaper. He tore the map into pieces to create a jigsaw puzzle. Then he asked his daughter to put the puzzle together again, thinking that she would spend a lot of time on the task, as a map was quite difficult for a six-year-old child to understand.

Within minutes, he was interrupted again. "Daddy, I am ready," his daughter exclaimed with pride. "This is incredible," said the father. "How did you do this so quickly?"

"It was so easy, Daddy," the little girl replied. "There is a beautiful woman on the back side of the paper. I just put her together, and the map was complete."

The girl did not care about the constraints of working with only one side of the page, and found a simple solution just by looking at the problem from a different perspective.

Mahatma Gandhi's granddaughter

Six-year-old girls are natural problem solvers.

Consider the story of little Ela, who visited her grandfather, Mahatma Gandhi, in his ashram (an Indian monastery) at the age of six. As her brother Arun Gandhi later remembered, the food at the ashram was just "terrible." Everyone's diet consisted of unsalted pumpkin for breakfast, lunch and dinner—the same boring food day in and day out. No-one questioned the menu, as everyone followed Gandhi's precept of eating simply.

Little Ela was fed up, however. "You should change the name of this place to Kola ashram!" she angrily said to her grandfather (kola is the Indian word for pumpkin). Gandhi was perplexed. "What do you mean, my child?" he asked. She explained that she was sick of getting nothing to eat but pumpkin.

It turned out that Gandhi was actually not fully aware of the situation. He only needed very little food himself, but never explicitly said that others should eat nothing but pumpkin. While he wanted them to eat simply, too, he did not mean for them to eat the same thing all of the time.

Gandhi quickly ordered other fruits and vegetables to be included in the simple meals that were prepared in the ashram, and little Ela was "the hero of the day."[2]

Ela was not held back by thoughts like "It has always worked like that," "We have tried that before," or "He would never approve that." She did not see the constraints that everyone else took for granted. She was not afraid to speak up and question the assumptions that no-one else questioned. This open-minded attitude enabled her to solve a problem that no adult in the ashram had been able to solve before.

You can do the same as little Ela did. If you are faced with a problem, just ask yourself what your assumptions are, and what constraints you (or others) see in that situation. Then question the assumptions and question the constraints. What if they weren't that important after all? And even if they might be, what could you do to overcome the constraints?

Divergent thinking

We can all learn from the wisdom of the six-year-old girls. Nothing and no-one held them back from trying out unconventional solutions. In fact, they just didn't care about the conventions (or didn't even know about them). With the right problem-solving mindset, they believed that problems are there be solved.

As a smart problem solver, you will allow yourself (and your team) to forget about constraints and suspend judgment—at least for a while. You will allow your mind to freely associate, look at problems from a completely different angle, and think the unthinkable. Some ideas might sound impossible to implement at first sight. Yet, they could already contain the seed of even better ideas that can help you to eventually solve the problem.

The process of exploring many different possible solutions for a problem is also called *divergent thinking*. This is not about playing safe and staying within some predetermined boundaries. It is not about succumbing to what other people (or your inner censor) say cannot be done. Divergent thinking means being open to exploring and imagining all types of possible solutions.

Of course, problem solvers also need the opposite of divergent thinking: *convergent thinking*. That's the type of more systematic thinking that leads from many possible answers to the one best answer. After all, in the end, you will most probably only be able to implement one solution for the problem rather than several solutions at the same time. But narrowing down to the one solution comes later in the process, in the 'Choose' stage (see Chapter 10). Before we can choose the best solution, we must first have several promising options to choose from.

So here's your task for the 'Create' phase: find as many potential solutions as possible (without judging them yet)!

Find people who know how to solve it

How do you find promising solutions then?

First of all, remember that you do not need to solve the problem alone. As we discussed in Chapter 5, being open to asking others for help in the problem-solving process is one of the key characteristics of people with a problem-solving mindset.

Other smart people might have solved the problem—or at least a similar one—before. Find them, and you will also get a big step closer to finding a solution.

So here is the first question to answer for smart solution finders:

Who has already found a way to handle such a problem?

Do you have a problem with your teenage child? You are for sure not alone. Other mothers and fathers have been through this before.

Do you feel stressed and overworked? Take a look at your colleagues who appear to be much less stressed. Ask them about their secret.

Do you have a problem in your business? Then you might check out whether another company has already found a way to deal with the issue that you are struggling with. Maybe you are getting complaints about a bad working climate in your company. What can you learn from other companies in your region who are winning best employer awards? Even when most of the companies in your industry are losing customers, where are the one or two positive exceptions that are still growing? Find the positive outliers and think about what can you learn from them.

Looking for 'best practices' is one way of filling your basket with solutions. But beware not to look only in the most obvious places. Look for ideas outside of the immediate domain, too.

Johannes Gutenberg had a printing press problem. He found a solution—a screw press—through copying how olive oil and wine presses worked (maybe a glass of wine also helped him to oil his thinking process).

Henry Ford had a car-production problem. He found a solution in designing an assembly line that was inspired by how butchers divided their work in animal 'disassembly' lines in the meat packing industry.

A hospital in England had a mortality problem in congenital heart disease surgeries. The doctors found the solution in a most unlikely place: in a partnership with the Formula One team of Ferrari.

It turned out in an in-depth investigation of root causes that the most critical risk factor for the surgeries was the transfer of patients between the operating room and the intensive care unit. It was not a surgery problem but a switchover problem. And who is an expert in fast switchovers? Formula One teams!

Ferrari had immense expertise from their pit-stops in Formula One races, and the Ferrari team helped the doctors develop a four-stage handover process for the surgical procedure. The new methodology also included the 'lollipop man' from the pit-stop: one person who is in charge of ensuring that all necessary tasks are completed in the right way (the anesthetist became the 'lollipop man' in the surgery process). As a result of the cooperation with Ferrari, the hospital significantly reduced errors in the handover process and improved patient safety.[3]

If you are looking for solutions, you do not necessarily need to find someone who has already solved exactly the same problem. It can almost be as useful to look for people who solved a similar kind of problem before.

For that purpose, go through the following two steps:

1. Think about whether you could describe your problem in a more abstract or general way (e.g. 'a fast switchover' instead of 'transferring patients from an operating room to an intensive care unit').
2. Ask who else—especially outside of your own domain or industry—could have already solved such a kind of problem.[4]

When you have identified the right people, see if you can find some information about how they solved the problem or—even better—

approach them directly and ask for advice. You will be surprised by how many people feel flattered about being asked for advice, and will then also be willing to help.

Before you ask, however, make sure that you know exactly what you want to ask for. Write a brief interview guideline with the most important questions that you would like to ask. Such a guideline will help you to focus the conversation on what really matters. A former McKinsey consultant advised closing every interview with what he calls "every McKinsey-ites favorite question: Is there anything else that I forgot to ask?"[5]

Look for other people who can help you to solve your problem—ask friends, experts, or your colleagues during the lunch break for advice. You won't always end up with a Ferrari solution, but it is for sure a fast way of generating new ideas that will potentially solve your problem.

Brainstorming reloaded

In addition to observing or asking outsiders and learning from their problem-solving strategies, you can also use creativity techniques to come up with potential solutions in your own team.

"Let's do some brainstorming"—that's what you often hear in today's organizations when there is a problem to solve. As a smart problem solver, you will be suspicious of that reflex!

The concept of brainstorming has been around for quite a while. Alex Osborn developed the group creativity method in the 1950s. Bring people together, ask them to put all possible ideas that they can come up with (including the wildest ones) on the table, and let them associatively build on each other's ideas without criticism—that's how brainstorming typically works. "Defer judgment" and "go for quantity" (as quantity is supposed to yield quality) are two ground rules of this creativity method.[6]

The idea sounds compelling. Just lock yourself in a room together with others, do some brainstorming—and voilà, here are the great ideas that will solve your problem.

There's a little problem with brainstorming, however. The results of several research studies are questioning its efficiency and effectiveness. Some people can dominate the discussion, others will put in less effort in a group situation, and some might fear looking foolish when they make very creative suggestions.[7] This means the results are not as good as they could be.

But here is the good news: brainstorming can still be useful—if you are aware of the method's limitations and if you do it in the right way:[8]

1. *Let the members of your team work individually first.* This will likely be a much more attractive method for coming up with solutions for more introverted people, and it can also mitigate some of the negative social effects of the group situation.

2. *Let people discuss their ideas in small groups.* Three to five people are enough. Many people are more comfortable exchanging ideas in a small group, and it is also possible to filter out very similar ideas in this way.

3. *Take a break!* Researchers have found that incubation time—the time in which you attend to other tasks and let ideas 'sink in'—can have a very positive effect on creative performance (see Chapter 4 on using the power of your unconscious mind).

4. *Then—and only then—start with your group discussion,* in which a facilitator takes ideas one by one and records them on a board or screen that all participants can focus on. When everyone has contributed their ideas, let them refine or build on the ideas of others. Make sure that people do not interrupt others or criticize their ideas—the evaluation of ideas will come at a later point in time (as part of the 'Choose' phase).

Alternatively, try to use *reverse brainstorming* to come up with creative solutions. Just ask "How can we cause the problem?" instead of "How can we solve the problem?"

Let us suppose you want ideas for how to make your company the most attractive employer in your region. Instead, ask the question "What could we do to become the least attractive employer?" Once you have brainstormed ideas for 'solving' this reverse problem, flip your solutions around to identify new ideas for solving the real problem.[9]

A similar approach is also used in the 'kill-the-company' exercise, in which you put yourself into the shoes of a competitor with unlimited resources and the courage to break all conventions, with the aim of putting you out of business. From thinking about what they would do, you can learn what you have to change to protect your business and successfully differentiate from the competition.[10]

Idea generation techniques for lonesome cowboys (and cow-girls)

You don't have a team at hand, and you also can't think of someone who can help you to solve the problem? Don't worry. Remember that the two six-year-old girls were able to solve their problems on their own.

Here are some techniques that you can use as a 'lonesome cowboy' (or a 'lonesome cowgirl') to come up with fresh ideas for solving a problem:

- **The logic tree.** We came across this tool in Chapter 8. A logic tree can be used for more than just identifying the root causes of a problem: it can also be used for developing a variety of potential solutions.[11] Let us take the 'most attractive employer' example from before. You could start with categorizing your ideas for solving the problem in a logic tree. Then work through the branches of the tree to see if you can come up with different ideas in the existing categories. (You might also decide you want to go back and add new categories to the first 'branch' of the tree.) This will give you a structured overview of the options that you have for solving the problem (see Figure 7).
- **The mind map.** This is another smart way of visualizing potential solutions in a diagram. Put the problem statement (or a picture or word that represents it) in the center of a blank page. Draw at least four or five branches that radiate out from the central statement or image. At the end of each of these branches, write down some ideas or keywords that come to mind about potential solutions. For each of these keywords, think about further associations that come to mind. Use these associations to add sub-branches with additional ideas. This tool will help you to quickly generate ideas and explore new pathways that you haven't thought about before. The great thing about mind mapping is that it mirrors how our brain works—with associations. A good mind map will help you to make and recognize connections between different ideas that you haven't seen before.

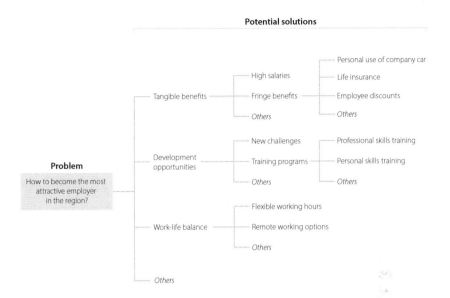

Figure 7 Example of a logic tree for generating ideas for solving a problem

- **The thought experiment.** In a thought experiment, we use our imagination to set up a fictional scenario in which we then try something out. Albert Einstein was a master of thought experiments. As a teenager, he imagined chasing after a beam of light. He later thought about what it would be like to measure light from a moving train.[12] These thought experiments were important milestones on the way to formulating his theory of special relativity. "I hold it true," said Einstein, "that pure thought can grasp reality."[13] We can all follow Einstein's example by imagining hypothetical situations in which we find answers to questions like "What would happen if ...?" or "What would it look like if ...?" (A thought experiment for overcoming a bad working climate in a company could, for example, start with the question "What would it look like if this were by far the best workplace in the country?")
- **Daydreaming.** Don't forget to use the power of your unconscious mind (Chapter 4). Do not force it when you cannot think of any more ideas for solving your problem. Relax and take a walk instead,

listen to your favorite music, meditate, visit an art museum, or go to a nearby café. If you have done some conscious problem-solving work beforehand, your mind will already be primed. Grant it the incubation time that it needs to develop new associations and come up with new solutions.[14]

- **Your own role.** Some problems seem to be difficult to solve because we locate them outside of our circle of influence (remember our discussion about this in Chapter 3?). One way to come closer to solving a problem is to bring it into your circle of influence. On the one hand, you might want to ask: *How do I contribute to the problem with my own behavior?* (Think about constant fights with family members or frequently having your proposals rejected by your boss as possible examples where this question might be useful for finding a solution).[15] On the other hand, you can also ask whether you can at least solve part of the problem on your own, even when it is impossible for you to solve the complete problem without the participation of others. You might not be able to change your boss, but maybe you could change the way you react or think about your boss's grumpy behavior. If you cannot change the whole system, can you change a small part of it, or if even that's not possible then can you at least find a way to be less affected by it?

These tools can help you to think about potential solutions. In the end, however, problem solving is not only a thinking process. Problems are solved through taking action. Smart problem solvers will therefore always look for solutions that are actionable and over which they have some influence. We'll look at how to pick the 'best' solutions in the next chapter.

If six-year-old girls can come up with smart solutions, I'm confident that you can do so too!

A little bit of science ...
on finding innovative solutions for tricky problems

- Researchers from British Columbia conducted two studies—one with creative experts and another one with undergraduate students—in which the participants were asked to list their sources of inspiration for their creative outputs. In both studies, influences from other domains (e.g. from music for technology) were more widespread than sources of inspiration from within the same domain.[16] Similar results were found by researchers from the US who concluded that "'outside the box' information stimulates a greater level of novelty when generating and refining creative ideas."[17]

- Researchers gave people the task to imagine life on other planets. When they received instructions that were formulated in a very specific way (e.g. 'think of specific animals that might be similar to the ones you'd find on Earth'), there was much less novelty in their creations than when the task was formulated in a more abstract way (e.g. 'think of environmental conditions or general survival needs'). The researchers concluded that there is a link between abstraction and novelty.[18]

- Research tells us what is needed for idea generation in groups to function well. Group members need to carefully pay attention to the ideas of others and give other group members enough time to reflect after the exchange of ideas (for example by incorporating an incubation period).[19] Letting people work independently first before they share their ideas in a group can lead to better-quality ideas than traditional brainstorming sessions.[20] Creativity training can help, too. It was found that groups trained in the use of creativity techniques (for example, working on idea generation and determining solutions in distinct phases) tended to find more creative solutions.[21]

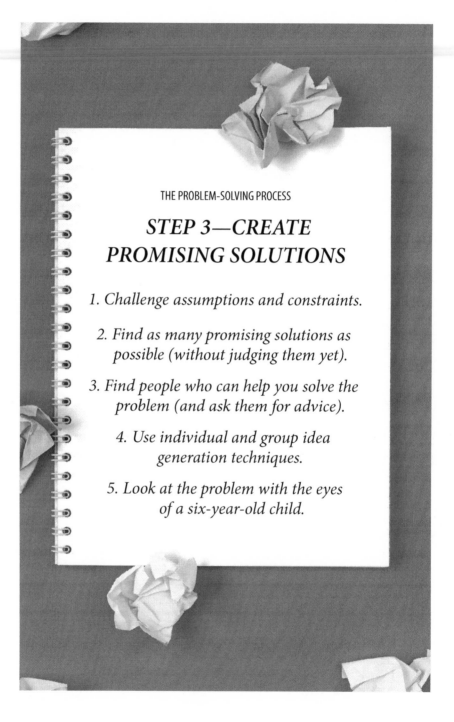

THE PROBLEM-SOLVING PROCESS

STEP 3—CREATE PROMISING SOLUTIONS

1. Challenge assumptions and constraints.

2. Find as many promising solutions as possible (without judging them yet).

3. Find people who can help you solve the problem (and ask them for advice).

4. Use individual and group idea generation techniques.

5. Look at the problem with the eyes of a six-year-old child.

CREATE SEVERAL PROMISING SOLUTIONS

Overcoming assumptions and constraints

What are the main assumptions/constraints?	Ways to overcome the constraints	What this means for potential solutions

People who can help

Who has already solved that kind of problem?	Who else could help to solve the problem?

Ideas for solutions

Advice/ideas from other people	Ideas from brainstorming with others	Ideas from individual idea-generation work

Figure 8 Create several promising solutions tool

10

Choose:
Decide on the optimal solution

Ward Clapham had the same problem that police officers from all around the world are typically faced with: how to curb crime in his district (in his case in Richmond, Canada).

There are several potential solutions to this problem: enhancing surveillance, educating the local population in crime prevention strategies, or increasing police presence in hot spots, to name just a few options. Boosting your efforts to "hunt down criminals—chase bad guys, kick in doors, get the bust"[1] is another option, one that the Canadian police officer was quite familiar with.

But Clapham eventually decided to follow a different path, saying that "we had to pull out of our reactive mode of waiting for youth to commit a crime before we intervened."[2] He explained how he came up with a completely new idea—issuing positive tickets.

The police officers in Richmond began to organize coupons for free food, movie tickets or other goodies that their typical clientele valued. Then they went out and rewarded the good behavior of local kids—for example, using the crosswalks, wearing helmets while biking, or speaking respectfully—with positive tickets.

The positive tickets not only reinforced the good behavior, they opened the door for the police and kids to develop a better relationship. The kids now began to see police officers in a different light. They were no longer seen as hunters who wanted to catch them in doing something illegal, but rather as people who cared. The kids no longer ran away when they saw a police officer. Youths who once stood at the edge of crime were now much further away from it, recognized Clapham with pride, "because he or she made a friend with one of my officers through positive tickets."[3]

The results of this initiative were impressive. Youth-related crime strongly decreased in the district, and positive tickets have been handed out with equally great success in many other communities, too. With the optimistic mindset of a smart problem solver, Clapham has obviously found the right solution for his problem.

Does the 'right' solution exist?

After you have created several ideas for solving a problem, it is time to choose the right one. This is when smart problem solvers switch from divergent to convergent thinking—the type of reasoning that narrows a range of options down to the one optimal solution.

In most problem situations, this is not an easy task. Many problems are problems exactly because there is no obvious best solution. There are often trade-offs involved, with drawbacks to every potential solution.

Think about the situation that Ward Clapham was in. Positive ticketing was by no means a widely acknowledged solution for crime prevention when he started the initiative. There were also risks involved. What if it didn't work out as planned? What if the kids didn't want to take the tickets from a police officer? He could have been accused of neglecting 'real' police work as he spent his time organizing movie tickets instead of chasing and arresting thugs.

In retrospect, it is always easy to say that a decision was 'right' or 'wrong,' because we can see the positive or negative outcomes that it caused. For most important decisions, however, you do not know the outcome in advance (otherwise there wouldn't be a decision to be made in the first place).

Reinhard K. Sprenger, a well-known German author of management books, provides the following example: think about a group of stone-age people fleeing from a saber-toothed tiger. There is a fork in the path ahead of them. "Take the left path!" some people cry. "No, to the right!"

cries another voice from behind. Both paths lead into unknown territory. There is no information about whether either path will be a deadly impasse or the road to safety. There is no 'right' or 'wrong' solution here—at least not at the point when the decision needs to be taken.[4]

A smart decision maker will first gather all the information that will enable them to make a well-informed decision (are there any signs of further dangerous animals ahead?). But quite often, the information about what will happen is just not available, as the future is inherently uncertain.

Let us keep this in mind when we look for the 'right' solution. We will often not be able to say what is really 'right' at the point in time when we make the decision. The outcomes of our decisions can differ from what we planned or hoped for. In this case, smart problem solvers will not say that they failed. With their growth mindset (see Chapter 2), they will see it as a learning opportunity instead, and as a new situation in which they can again look for the best possible solution. (Well, maybe the saber-toothed tiger would not have given us this second chance, but luckily these predators have become quite rare during the last 12,000 years.)

Create a shortlist of the most promising solutions

Smart problem solvers will acknowledge that the perfect 'right' solution is hard to find. If it existed, we would probably not be faced with the problem at all. What smart problem solvers do instead is to strive for an *optimal solution*. This is the most favorable solution under a specific set of circumstances; the solution that brings you closest to meeting your most important goals even if you are not able to completely meet *all* your goals.

So how do you identify the optimal solution for your problem then?

The first step is to create a shortlist of the best ideas for solving the problem. Thanks to the 'Create' phase (see Chapter 9), you have probably already identified a whole bunch of different ideas. Large choice sets are quite difficult to handle, however, and exploring all the pros and cons of dozens of different options can just be overwhelming. With a more limited number of choices, you will have more time to evaluate which of the solutions is the optimal one.

There are three steps you can take to reduce the number of potential solutions to a more manageable quantity:[5]

1. *Cluster your ideas*—some solutions will be quite similar, so you can group them together. Again, a logic tree might help you to approach this task in a structured way.
2. *Prioritize* the (clustered) solutions in terms of their *potential impact*. If the solution works, how confident are you that it will solve your problem (e.g. on a simple scale of *low impact, medium impact* or *high impact*)?
3. Assess *how easy or difficult it will be to implement your solution*, for example in terms of the costs and efforts required, or the level of commitment or resistance that you are likely to meet from others (on a scale from *easy to implement* to *difficult to implement*). Keep in mind that you will most probably need the buy-in of other people who are involved in the problem situation to eventually make your solution work.

You can use a simple two-dimensional I^2 *matrix* (I^2 stands for *impact* and *implementation*) to evaluate the possible solutions that you found based on points 2 and 3 above (see Figure 9). The solutions that have a high potential impact and are relatively easy to implement will be your favorite candidates for solving the problem.

Ideally, you will not have more than three to six promising solutions left on your shortlist before you proceed to the next stage, in which you select the optimal solution.[6]

Time to decide

Take your shortlist of the most promising solutions, revisit the goals that you set in the 'Clarify' phase (see Chapter 7), and get ready to make a decision.

Here's what smart problem solvers will do to get from three to five potential options for solving a problem to the optimal one.

First, they will evaluate each of the options in more detail:

1. *Write down the pros and cons for each option.* What are the likely positive and negative outcomes of a solution? What are its strengths

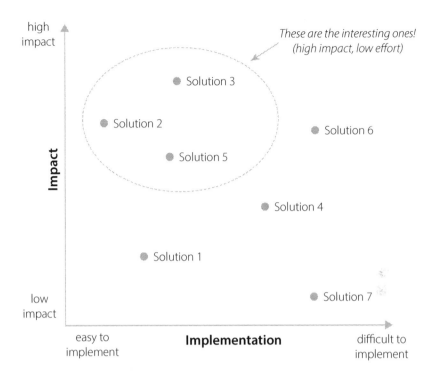

high impact

These are the interesting ones!
(high impact, low effort)

Impact

⬤ Solution 3

⬤ Solution 2

⬤ Solution 6

⬤ Solution 5

⬤ Solution 4

⬤ Solution 1

low impact

⬤ Solution 7

easy to
implement

Implementation

difficult to
implement

Figure 9 Example of an I² matrix

and weaknesses? It might sound simple, but taking your time to think through what speaks for and against each solution will help you to gain more clarity about which solutions have a higher chance of leading to a favorable outcome.

2. *Weigh the pros and cons.* Not every argument about the strengths and weaknesses of a proposed solution has the same weight. Think about which of the points on your pros and cons list are more or less important for you—you can then rate them on a scale of '+' to '+++' on the positive side and '–' to '– – –' on the negative side.[7]

3. *Create a best-case and a worst-case scenario.* What's the best that can happen when you choose this solution? And what would happen in the worst case? If you know the answers to these two questions, you will make your hopes and fears explicit, which can further help

you to judge which of the options potentially have more upsides or downsides than the others.

After conducting these evaluations, you should have a good understanding of the relative advantages and disadvantages of each of the proposed solutions. In most cases, some options will already stand out.

Now it is really time to make your decision. Remember, this is not about finding the 'right' or 'wrong' solution, but about identifying the optimal one—the one that helps to get you closest to your goals.

This is why you need to take a close look at your goals again (see Chapter 7). What do you actually want to achieve? What are the ideal and 'good enough' outcomes for you? And what are the goals of other parties who are also involved in the problem situation?

You can then carefully judge to what extent each of the suggested solutions will help you to reach your goals. Choose the one that brings you closest to achieving them.

Of course, there might be a trade-off involved. One solution will help you achieve one goal but miss another. In that case, take a second look at which of the conflicting goals is more important for you. Choose the option that brings you closest to the goals that you value the most.

Taking a second look

Have you made a decision? That's great! If you followed all the steps outlined above, you should be quite confident that you have found the optimal solution for your problem.

If you are not one hundred percent confident yet, you might want to make some final checks before fully committing yourself to implementing the solution:

- **The information check.** Do you really have all the information that you need to take the decision? If not, or if you are unsure about the quality of the available data, could you still obtain additional information that would make you more confident in your decision?
- **The sunk cost check.** Are you making your decision based on what you want to achieve in the future rather than what you did in the

past? Some people tend to succumb to what is known as the 'sunk cost effect.' They still cling to certain things because they hate to give up on something they've already put a lot of effort into. Investing more money in a project that turned out to be a failure is one example. Continuing to watch a bad movie just because you've already bought a cinema ticket is another one. Are you sure that you are not preferring a solution just because you have already invested a lot of time and money into something that is actually not working well? Make sure to consider only future benefits and costs in your choices. "The rest of your life begins now," advises psychologist Richard Nisbett in his book about smart thinking. "Nothing that happened yesterday can be retrieved. No use crying over spilt milk."[8]

- **The sensitivity (or 'what if') check.** You'll have made some assumptions about the outcomes of implementing your preferred solution. Ask yourself what would happen if things turned out differently than you currently foresee. What if that person reacts differently? What if you don't get the support that you think you'll get? What if your competitor launches a similar product in the market before you? When you have answered your 'what if' questions, is the preferred option still viable?

- **The 'no regrets' check.** If you are like most other decision makers, you will want to avoid your decision leading to severe negative outcomes that you would later regret.[9] Therefore, take a look at your worst-case scenario for your preferred solution. Have you considered all possible negative consequences? Are there any ramifications—for example between your work life and private life—that you haven't yet thought of? If you consider the potential negative consequences, will you be able to cope with them? You could then devise an action plan for avoiding or addressing the negative consequences of your decision.

The additional checks can help you to become more confident that you chose the right solution. But beware! They can also nourish your doubts.

In this case, remind yourself that the perfect decision does not exist—and that not taking a decision will also have its own consequences. When Bronnie Ware, an Australian nurse who worked in palliative care for a long time, studied what people regret the most when they are close to dying, these regrets were primarily about not having done something (such as not having the courage to live a life true to themselves, not staying in touch with friends, or not allowing themselves to express their feelings). They rarely regret having made a tough decision.[10]

This brings us to the last—and most important—check to help you with your final decision: the 'heart check.'

The 'heart check'

I'm not speaking about a medical heart check up here, but about listening to what your heart says about the decision.

We've done a lot of brain work in this chapter to logically derive the optimal solution from a broader range of possible solutions. But is the optimal solution also the one that you can stand behind with all your heart?

Here are a few questions that you can ask yourself when you have a difficult decision to make (in addition to the checks that we have already discussed):[11]

- **The fear question: "What are you afraid of?"** Is there a fear that is holding you back from adopting a certain solution? Are you afraid of failure, of disappointing someone else, of disappointing yourself? Although fears are usually not our best guides, it can be helpful to make them explicit. We can then either think about how we could overcome the fears, or whether the fears tell us something important about the decision we are about to make.
- **The purpose question: "What's the real purpose behind this?"** This question invites you to think about the bigger picture. What do you actually want to achieve in your life—and how would your decision contribute to your 'end goals'? Let us assume that your end goal is to spend a lot of time with your loved ones; you would like to accompany your children during their golden childhood years. Is accepting the highly paid consulting job in which you will need to travel four to five days every week really the right choice then? Thinking about the purpose that you see in your life, does your decision reflect what you want to achieve and who you want to be?

- **The beneficiary question: "Who are you doing this for?"** That is the most common regret that Bronnie Ware observed when she interviewed the dying—they wished they had lived a life true to themselves instead of just living the life that others expected of them.[12] It is of course a good idea to keep the interests of others in mind when you make your decisions. Smart problem solvers will always seek a solution that benefits both others and themselves. But when the pendulum swings too much in one direction—if you forget your own needs over your eagerness to please others—you might end up with regrets rather than with a good solution.
- **The look-in-the-mirror question: "How will it feel when you look in the mirror?"** This question forces you to think about how you will feel about yourself when you have made your choice. Will you be able to look at yourself in the mirror and say "Yes, this was the right thing to do, and I can fully stand behind it"? Or will you end up not liking yourself because of your decision? Think about how this decision will make you feel once you are confronted with the consequences. Will you feel content with yourself?
- **The heart question: "What does your heart say about it?"** Even if the solution that you found makes perfect sense from a rational, analytic point of view—does it feel right for you, too? Forget what others say for a moment. Forget about all the conventions, about what you 'must' or 'should' do. Digging deeper, what is it that you really believe in? What feels like the right thing to do?

These questions should help you to make the right choice, the one that you can wholeheartedly say "Yes" to.

Sometimes when you have a big decision to make in your life, you will take more time to carefully think through your options. In other cases, the solution will emerge more intuitively, as in the case of our two six-year-old problem solvers from the last chapter. In all cases, however, you will make a better choice when you think logically with your mind, but at the same time consider what your heart says.

The secret of smart problem solvers is to listen well in order to be able to decide well. As Ward Clapham says, "not just listen with your ears—but listen with your heart and your eyes."[13]

A little bit of science ...
on making the right choice

- Do more options lead to better decisions? Not necessarily. Researchers have found that people who choose from a smaller number of options tend to be more satisfied with their choice than those who sacrifice a lot of time and resources evaluating a large number of options.[14] Those who choose from a wider set of options are especially more prone to worrying about what they have missed out on from not having gone with another option.[15]
- The more time we have already invested in an activity, the more likely we are to pursue it further—even if there is no indication that we will ever be able to succeed. This tendency of overrating sunk costs was actually found not only in humans, but also in mice and rats.[16] If you want to be smarter than mice and rats, think about the future when you make your decisions, and not about what you have already invested in the past.
- Several research studies confirm that anticipated regret is an important factor in determining our choices.[17] In one study, 108 people were asked to use a diary to rate their expected and experienced regrets in decision making. They forecasted regret for 70 percent of their future decisions, but actually experienced regret in only 30 percent of their decisions.[18] So even though there is a chance that you will regret a decision, it is probably lower than you think.

THE PROBLEM-SOLVING PROCESS

STEP 4—CHOOSE THE OPTIMAL SOLUTION

1. Create a shortlist of the most promising solutions (potential impact and ease of implementation).

2. Weigh the pros and cons and choose the option that bring you closest to your goals.

3. Make some last checks before taking a final decision (information check, sunk cost check, sensitivity check, 'no regrets' check, heart check).

4. Don't forget to listen to what your heart says.

CHOOSE THE OPTIMAL SOLUTION

1 Prioritize potential solutions (I² matrix)

2 Evaluate the options

Option	Pros*	Cons*	Best case	Worst case
Solution 2				
Solution 3				
Solution 5				

* Note: First describe and then weigh the pros a pros and cons by their importance on a scale of '+' to '+++' (for pros) and '–' to '–––' (for cons)

3 Preferred option

4 Take a second look

- ◯ Information check
- ◯ Sunk cost check
- ◯ **'Heart check'**
- ◯ 'No regrets' check
- ◯ 'What if' check

Figure 10 Choose the optimal solution tool

11

Commit: Make it happen

You will find many smart problem solvers among entrepreneurs. One salient example is James Dyson, who built a billion-dollar business based on solving a housecleaning problem.[1]

Dyson was frustrated with existing vacuum cleaners that tended to push dirt around the room instead of sucking it up. He decided to solve the problem.

The solution that he came up with was a thing called a cyclonic separator. He had seen such a device in a sawmill, where it was used for removing dust from the air. He thought that this might also work in a vacuum cleaner.

By this point, Dyson had already proceeded through the first four steps of the problem-solving process. He clarified which problem he wanted to solve and set his goals ('Clarify'), he identified the cause of the problem (the poor suction of the existing vacuum cleaner technology) ('Causes'), he looked for potential solutions ('Create'), and he chose the most promising solution for the problem—the cyclonic separator ('Choose').

There's only one phase in the problem-solving process left now—committing to implementing the idea. And Dyson was indeed committed. "I became obsessed," he later remembered. "It took five years of doing nothing but making and testing prototypes."[2]

He actually made 5,127 prototypes altogether. Most people thought he was mad, but his wife continued to support him. While he was busy tyring out one prototype after another, she earned the family income with her art teaching.

Despite many setbacks on the way, Dyson did not give up. With the right problem-solving mindset—including a strong belief in his ability to overcome challenges—he eventually succeeded in coming up with a model that worked.

He then planned to sell his new invention to the domestic appliances industry, but they did not want it. A licensing agreement with Amway ended in disaster. As a last resort, he decided to set up his own manufacturing company. He risked losing his house when he borrowed the money to make it happen.

Fortunately, the house remained in his ownership as the vacuum cleaners began to sell like crazy. That problem-solving process was the beginning of an exceptional entrepreneurial success story.

Making progress in loops

As we can see from James Dyson's story, implementing a solution—as good as it looks at first sight—is not always straightforward. There will be obstacles. We need to expect complications. Not everything will always work out as planned.

Being fully committed to following through with a solution—just as James Dyson was with his cyclonic vacuum cleaner—is an important precondition for eventually being able to solve a problem. You need to be persistent, and optimistic that you will eventually be able to solve the problem. Many problems are not solved on the first attempt, and perseverance is often the key to success (though luckily, most problems don't require over five thousand attempts before they are solved).

The trick of smart problem solvers is to understand the iterative nature of the implementation process. It is usually not a straight line that immediately leads to success, but instead a series of learning loops (see Figure 11).

Each loop consists of four phases:

1. **Plan.** Develop an action plan of how you will implement your solution.
2. **Test.** Try things out without expecting that everything will work perfectly right away.

3. **Review.** Take a step back and check whether it worked or not.
4. **Learn.** Modify your solution based on what you have learned.

Dyson went through a lot of learning loops. He planned one prototype after another, tested them, reviewed the outcomes, and then learned what to change in order to get another step ahead.

For example, he planned to sell licenses to manufacturers of household appliances, tested his approach (offering a deal to the manufacturers), reviewed the outcome (the deal was refused), learned from the failure, and succeeded in another way (setting up his own manufacturing company). "I got to a place I never could have imagined because I learned what worked and didn't work,"[3] he said in an interview with the *Entrepreneur* magazine.

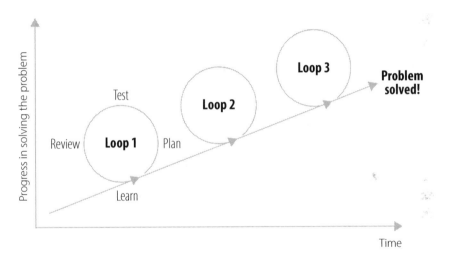

Figure 11 Making progress through learning loops

Plan–Test–Review–Learn—with each loop, you are getting closer to solving your problem.[4]

Let us now take a closer look at the four phases of the learning loop.

Plan and test

If you are committed to a promising solution for your problem, you first need to break it down into actionable steps in order to really get things done.

Making a plan means translating a big idea into concrete tasks. This is how it works: visualize the ideal outcome (the *end goal*) first. Then think about which milestones (or *intermediate goals*) you could set yourself on the way. Then list the tasks you (or others who could help you to implement the solution) will need to accomplish to get there.

It is always a combination of small steps that enables us to achieve our big goals. Only having a dream is not enough. We must also take action to make it come true.

Smart problem solvers therefore ask themselves:

- "Which tasks do I need to complete in the next three months to reach my goal?"
- "What do I need to do next week to make progress on these tasks?"
- "What will I do today to make it happen?"

Thus, they translate their idea into SMART tasks. That's a concept that you will likely have heard of before, but most probably related to goals rather than tasks.

SMART goals (and tasks) are specific (so you know exactly what you want to achieve), measurable (so you know when you are making progress), achievable, relevant for solving the problem, and time-based (with a clear deadline).

Although the concept is basically the same, I prefer the term 'task' in the context of committed problem solving. Whereas a goal is more about what you would *like* to achieve, a task is about what you actually *must do* and *will do*. After all, it is concrete action rather than abstract goals that will solve your problem.

"I will go to the gym to lose weight" is not formulated in a SMART way, for example. It is not very specific and measurable, and a clear timeline is missing, too. "I will go to the gym three days a week for the next six months with the aim of decreasing my weight by 10 pounds" is a much SMARTer way of formulating the task. Now we'll know whether or not we are able to successfully implement our task.

Your action plan will include all the tasks that you (or others in your support team) are committed to completing, and a timeline that indicates when you want to complete them.

When the action plan is ready, it is time for testing.

Testing means implementing your plan—with confidence that it will work, but at the same time being open to proving yourself wrong. Smart problem solvers do not assume that everything will always work out just as planned. With a growth mindset (see Chapter 2), they are willing to fail, learn from failure, and try again. "Failure is interesting," says James Dyson. "It's part of making progress."[5]

Beware, however: the reason for conducting 'live tests' is not "to confirm what we believe is true,"[6] but to find out what works and what doesn't in solving our problem.

Review and learn

We can find out more about what works and what doesn't when we take some time to review the outcome of our actions.

Did everything work out as planned? That's great—it seems that you are on the right path for solving your problem (don't forget to celebrate the progress you've made!).

Did things not work out as planned? That's great, too—because this is your chance to learn. Did you make any wrong assumptions that you need to correct? Did you meet some unexpected obstacles? Did you overlook something? Try to understand what happened and why. This is your path to progress.

Problem solving is not about forcing things. Smart problem solvers with a growth mindset understand that it is a learning process.

Learning on the way means that you not only remain open to changing your approach, but also to modifying your goals. When you fail to make progress, do not simply ask yourself what else you could do to reach your goal. Ask whether you could (or should) adjust your goals, too. Why did you set that goal in the first place? Is it still that important for you? Or could you maybe just let go of a particular goal and find a better one instead?

Learning is a never-ending process of planning, trying out new things, and adjusting your approach—and maybe also your goals—on the way.

Successful entrepreneurs understand how this learning process works. Take Sara Blakely, the founder of Spanx, as another example. She is the youngest self-made female billionaire in the world. Where did this incredible success come from?

When she was a child, her father used to sit down with her at the kitchen table and ask: "What did you fail at this week?"[7] He did not ask about all the A's that she received in school, or about the goals that she scored in the soccer team. He asked his daughter what she learned from failing. And when she told him about the failure of the week, he gave her a high five. They celebrated the learning loop together. As Blakely later said in an interview with Fortune, "My dad taught me that failing simply just leads you to the next great thing."[8]

Get the commitment of others

Remember what we discussed in Chapter 5 about the mindset of smart problem solvers? You do not need to solve problems on your own.

Sara Blakely had her father as a mentor on her side, and James Dyson may not have sold a single vacuum cleaner without the support of his wife. We all need other people to help us succeed in life.

In most problem situations, you just need a few committed people on your side. As Margaret Mead allegedly said, "Never doubt that a small group of thoughtful, committed citizens can change the world. Indeed, it is the only thing that ever has."[9]

So don't forget to rally your support team to make things happen. Think about who needs to buy in, and remember that people are usually more inclined to join you when you include them in the decision-making process. "Even if you have great solutions," explains leadership expert John C. Maxwell, "you can fail to solve a problem if people haven't bought in."[10]

To get the engagement of other people, you first need to build a good relationship with them. People need to feel that they are important to you, that you are listening to them, and that you value their opinion on how to solve the problem. Give them the feeling of being in a partnership, of being "up to something together."[11] Instead of just presenting final solutions, involve them in your problem-solving journey. And don't forget that building the relationship is as important as taking concrete action to solve the problem.

So let us summarize what you will need to successfully implement a solution for your problem:

- Commit yourself to taking action.
- Build relationships and engage your support team.
- Try things out and learn on the way.

It is important to thoroughly think about how to solve a problem, but the only way to actually solve it is through getting things done together with other people.

It will be easier with people you trust on your side. Then you can see problems as opportunities—to learn, to grow, and to improve—and to make life better than it was before the problem occurred. As James Dyson said, "Life is a mountain of solvable problems and I enjoy that."[12]

A little bit of science ...
on effectively implementing your solution

- Persistence—ongoing commitment to investing effort into solving a problem even when you face obstacles—is a key factor for being able to find and successfully implement a viable solution. Two researchers from Northwestern University who conducted seven studies on the topic came to the conclusion that "persistence is a critical determinant of creative performance and that people may undervalue and underutilize persistence in everyday creative problem solving."[13]
- K. Anders Ericsson, a Swedish psychologist and Professor of Psychology at Florida State University, conducted extensive research on how people become master problem solvers in different domains (including, for example, chess grandmasters or master surgeons). He found that these top-level experts had one thing in common: they put a lot of effort into what he called 'deliberate practice.'[14] This is planned and focused action in which they try out and practice new skills, get feedback about their performance, deliberately think about what worked and what didn't (and why), and then learn and adjust their next actions accordingly. The process through which expert problem solvers acquire their expertise is very similar to the learning loop (*Plan–Test–Review–Learn*) described in this chapter.
- Ericsson also found that people who become experts in their field are typically supported by more experienced professionals on the way.[15] We also know from the research on the positive outcomes of executive and life coaching how important the commitment and support of others can be for fostering people's ability to solve problems.[16]

THE PROBLEM-SOLVING PROCESS

STEP 5—COMMIT YOURSELF (AND OTHERS) TO MAKING YOUR SOLUTION WORK

1. If you have chosen your preferred solution, take action—try it out and learn on the way.

2. Many problems are not solved right away, but require going through several learning loops (Plan–Test–Review–Learn).

3. To solve a problem, you must first be committed to solving it—and then show persistence.

4. It is much easier to solve a problem with the support of other people who are committed to getting the problem solved too.

COMMIT YOURSELF (AND OTHERS) TO MAKING YOUR SOLUTION WORK

Your support team

Who can help you to implement your solution?   *What could they contribute?*

| Person 1 | |
| Person 2 | |

...

1 Plan

What will you do to implement your solution?   *Who?*   *By when?*

| Task 1 | | |
| Task 2 | | |

...

2 Test

Take action—try things out!

3 Review

➕   ➖

What worked well?   *Why?*   *What didn't work?*   *Why not?*

| | | | |
| | | | |

4 Learn

What should we do differently?

| |
| |

... and then start the next learning loop (start with 'Plan' again)

Figure 12 Commit yourself (and others) tool

Conclusion: Problem solved!

Congratulations on getting this far! Equipped with insights from the stories of smart problem solvers from Anne Sullivan and Helen Keller to Albert Einstein and James Dyson, with your new knowledge of the science of problem solving, and with a range of practical problem-solving tools in your personal toolbox, you should now be able to confidently tackle even the toughest problems.

You will remember that it always depends on both your mindset and your actions to find and implement the solutions that will improve your own life and the lives of others.

Maybe you will also see the smaller and bigger problems that you and others around you encounter in a different light now—as a learning opportunity that allows you to make progress and grow rather than a 'bad thing' that intrudes into your life.

As with physical muscles, your problem-solving muscle will be strengthened with practice and training. So let's get started! Try out the method and tools from this book on problems that you see in your professional or personal life, and on issues that you really care about for the community or our planet. Try them out, review the results, learn, and make progress on solving the problems that matter most to you.

The world needs more smart problem solvers. As the examples in this book show, these are the people who change the world. They shape the future by solving one problem after another, no matter how big or small.

As part of this community of smart problem solvers, you will tackle the right problems (those that are really important and where you can make a difference), find innovative solutions, and make the world around you a little better.

As we have repeatedly discussed in this book, it is usually easier to solve problems with other people by your side. So you might want to share this book with your colleagues, team members, students, friends, or family, too. If they become smart problem solvers just as you have, it will be much easier for you to jointly solve problems.

If you also feel that the world needs even more smart problem solvers, I would be very grateful if you could write a short honest online review for this book. With every extra person who knows how to become a smart problem solver, we will solve more and more problems.

Thank you for accompanying me on the journey of exploring how smart problem solvers think and act, and let me wish you all the best for your own problem-solving endeavors.

"A journey of three thousand miles begins with one step,"[1] wrote the legendary Chinese philosopher Lao-Tze. To solve a problem, you must take the first step too.

The problem-solving process on one page

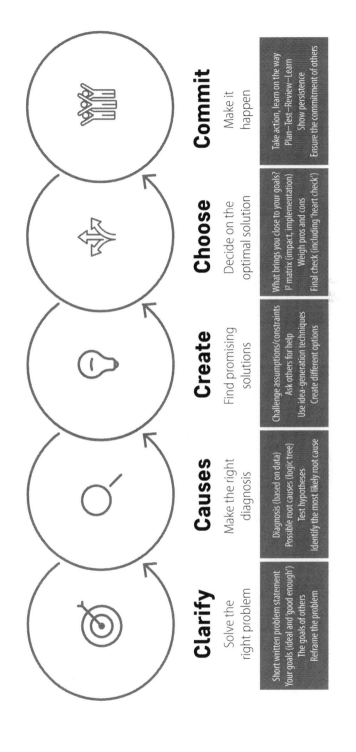

Clarify
Solve the right problem

Short written problem statement
Your goals (ideal and 'good enough')
The goals of others
Reframe the problem

Causes
Make the right diagnosis

Diagnosis (based on data)
Possible root causes (logic tree)
Test hypotheses
Identify the most likely root cause

Create
Find promising solutions

Challenge assumptions/constraints
Ask others for help
Use idea-generation techniques
Create different options

Choose
Decide on the optimal solution

What brings you close to your goals?
I² matrix (impact, implementation)
Weigh pros and cons
Final check (including 'heart check')

Commit
Make it happen

Take action, learn on the way
Plan—Test—Review—Learn
Show persistence
Ensure the commitment of others

Appendix:
Solve it like the pros

"One more thing"—that's what Steve Jobs, founder and former CEO of Apple (and a smart problem solver, too!)—used to say at the end of his keynote speeches before he would present another highlight of his company's innovative products (which have arguably solved the problems of millions of people who didn't even know that they had such a problem before).

I am not Steve Jobs, but I have also prepared "one more thing" for you here. Are you interested in digging deeper into how people who make a (really good) living from solving problems for other people approach the problem-solving task? Then you might want to take a look at the following pages and get further inspiration from how scientist, doctors, designers, consultants, expert negotiators and coaches solve problems in a highly professional way.

Solve it like a scientist

Scientists are often working on really big problems. Whether they are vaccine researchers trying to find a solution for combating a virus, environmental scientists developing strategies for reducing carbon dioxide emissions, or rocket scientists exploring how to make spaceflight possible—they are all masters of a particular problem-solving approach that is the basis for all scientific work.

Scientists typically start their problem-solving endeavor with a crystal clear and very specific research question. It is usually focused on a single problem or issue and provides a clear aim for the research—finding an answer to that question.

After clarifying the research aim, a scientist will take a look at what others have already found out about the problem. They check out journal articles and books that other academic experts in their field have already written about the topic, and then try to synthesize their findings in a review of what they call the 'state of the art' in the literature.

Then comes a very important step: based on what they found out about the problem, they will form a hypothesis (or, in many cases, several hypotheses). A hypothesis is a proposed explanation of how things might work, formulated in a way that makes it possible to test whether it is right or wrong. It is usually a statement about a relationship between two or more things. "Students who drink more alcohol on the night before an exam are more likely to get worse grades" is one example of a hypothesis.

Good scientists are not emotionally attached to their hypotheses and do not assume that they are true. A hypothesis is just the starting point for a closer investigation—a statement that can either be supported or falsified through gathering and analyzing data.

Once a hypothesis is formulated, the scientist will determine which data and method they could use to test it. Sometimes they use quantitative research methods, in which they collect and analyze numerical data, and at other times they use qualitative methods, which are focused on making sense of non-numerical data like words or pictures. Researchers create experiments, conduct interviews and surveys, make observations, analyze documents or other readily available data, or combine several methods in a 'mixed-methods' approach.

To test the hypothesis that we proposed above, researchers could, for example, conduct a survey among students to find out how much alcohol they drank on the night before the exam, and then look at how this correlates to their exam grades. They would usually also take 'control variables' into account in their analysis. These are other potential influences on the outcome (e.g. the number of hours that students studied for the exam or slept the night before it). Scientists study these other variables to make sure the variable they are interested in (in our case the alcohol consumption) is definitely the one that is having a significant impact on the outcome variable (the grades).

The analysis of the collected data will then reveal whether the hypothesis is supported or falsified. Both results are equally acceptable and important for a smart scientific problem solver. Falsification of a hypothesis might be unfortunate for the specific theory that a researcher wants to construct, but it is still helpful for advancing our common knowledge. At least we know what doesn't work. It is then time to set up a new hypothesis that will be tested again with appropriate data. That's how science—and mankind—is making progress.

But scientists also know that even if our hypotheses are supported, theories always remain provisional: "No matter how many times the results of experiments agree with some theory, you can never be sure that the next time the result will not contradict the theory,"[1] wrote the brilliant physicist Stephen Hawking. Good scientists always remain open to proving themselves wrong.

What smart problem solvers can learn from scientists

Work with hypotheses, find clever ways to test them with objective data, and always consider the possibility that your hypotheses might be wrong.

Solve it like a doctor

It is a doctor's job to solve medical problems. And we all know how a good doctor works: the therapy is based on a thorough diagnosis.

But what does a thorough diagnosis look like? When a patient comes to them with a health problem, doctors first gather information, which they then interpret to determine a working diagnosis.[2]

The doctor will consider different sources of information:

- A clinical history check, which might also look at risk factors in the family history
- An interview with the patient
- A physical exam
- Diagnostic tests (e.g. a blood test)
- Communication with the patient's family members
- The expertise of other physicians (they may also send the patient to specialized colleagues for referrals or consultations)

Doctors typically work in iterative cycles. That means that the working hypothesis is updated (or maybe abandoned) as more information is gathered, integrated, and interpreted.

Often, doctors will also make a differential diagnosis, which means that they develop several hypotheses about different potential conditions that could be causing the patient's symptoms. In this case, they would usually conduct several tests or gather more information to see which of their hypotheses they can confirm, and which ones they have to abandon.

Let us imagine that a patient is experiencing a persistent, strong headache. The doctor could have several conditions in mind, such as a migraine, headaches which occur from medication overuse, tension-type headaches, or post-traumatic headaches that develop after injuries. To refine the diagnosis, the doctor might check the patient's medication, or ask whether they had a head injury during the last few days. They might also want to rule out the possibility of a brain tumor or hemorrhage with additional MRI or CT scans.

To start with, the list of potential diagnoses is usually quite wide. With the integration of new information, the number of options will be narrowed in what is called diagnostic refinement. Once there are only one or two possibilities left, diagnostic refinement is replaced by diagnostic verification, in which the doctor checks whether the diagnosis really explains all symptoms and is coherent with the patient's context (e.g. their medical history or risk factors).

The doctor (or the diagnostic team) will always check whether they have collected enough information before they finally decide on a therapy. If this is not yet the case, the process of information gathering, integration and interpretation, and hypothesis building continues.

"It is important to note that clinicians do not need to obtain diagnostic certainty prior to initiating treatment," recommends the Committee on Diagnostic Error in Health Care. "The goal of information gathering in the diagnostic process is to reduce diagnostic uncertainty enough to make optimal decisions for subsequent care."[3]

What smart problem solvers can learn from doctors

Start a problem diagnosis with several different hypotheses in mind, then narrow down the number of options through gathering and interpreting additional information.

Solve it like a designer

When professional designers create new products and services, they often use a problem-solving approach that is now widely known by the term *design thinking*. It has been popularized especially by David M. Kelley, founder of the globally active design firm IDEO and of Stanford University's Hasso Plattner Institute of Design.

Similar to a doctor's diagnosis, design thinking is an iterative problem-solving process.

In this process, the designers do not assume that they already know everything that it takes to solve a problem from the beginning. Instead, they first try to understand the needs of the user for whom the designers—who usually work in diverse, interdisciplinary teams—develop new or improved products and services.

The design team then quickly comes up with first solutions ('prototypes'), which are directly tested with the users. Based on user feedback, the prototypes are revised and improved, and then again tested with the users. This cycle is repeated until both users and designers say "Yes, this is a great solution to our problem!"

Here are the five steps of the design thinking cycle:[4]

1. **Empathize:** Try to understand the users—interview them, observe them, and dig deeper to find out more about their needs.
2. **Define:** Craft a meaningful problem statement based on the users' needs.
3. **Ideate:** Generate a wide set of potential solutions for the problem. Use imagination and build on each other's ideas in a team. Make sure to separate idea generation from idea evaluation (do not curb creativity with criticism).
4. **Prototype:** Identify a promising solution and create 'something' that lets the user experience how it works. That 'something' could be a physical prototype (if it is quick and cheap to make), or perhaps a role-play activity (to experience a service) or a storyboard that visualizes the user experience in a series of illustrations.
5. **Test:** Present your prototype to the users and learn from their feedback. Do not explain everything but let them experience it. Observe how they react, and ask them how they feel about it. What do they like about your solution? What don't they like? You might also ask the user to compare different solutions in this phase.

With the feedback that you receive in the 'Test' phase (which should help you to better understand the user), you can go back to prior stages and come up with new ideas and refined prototypes. Maybe you'll even want to revise your problem statement.

Design thinking is not about linear progression. Designers make progress in iterative cycles (a bit like in the learning loops that we discussed in Chapter 11). They may fail on the way, but they usually fail quickly and cheaply.[5] Most importantly, they are staying in touch with the people whose problems they solve. Thus, they do not see problem solving as a one-time creative act, but as an ongoing conversation.

What smart problem solvers can learn from designers

Make progress by going through iterative cycles in which you test and refine your solutions together with the users.

Solve it like a consultant

When executives in large organizations face complex problems, they often hire management consultants. These are people who are highly skilled in problem-solving methods, and are usually also highly paid for applying these skills to solving organizational problems.

One of the most prestigious consulting firms is McKinsey & Company, founded in the 1920s by James O. McKinsey, a professor at the University of Chicago. The revenue of 'the firm,' as McKinsey is often called, exceeded 10 billion US dollars in 2019.[6] It's a really big problem-solving business.

Several current and former McKinsey consultants have written books about the firm's approach to problem solving. Rob McLean and Charles Conn are two of them. In their book *Bulletproof Problem Solving*, they describe a seven-step process that consultants use to solve complex problems:[7]

1. Define the problem (in a precise way)
2. Disaggregate—break the problem down into its component issues and develop hypotheses that you then explore further
3. Prioritize the issues—focus on the issues with the highest impact
4. Create a workplan—who is going to do what and by when
5. Gather and analyze data
6. Synthesize your findings—summarize your main insights
7. Communicate your findings in a compelling story

One of the main ideas here is not trying to solve everything at the same time, but first taking the problem apart "into logical pieces"[8] (that's what 'disaggregate' means here). The prime work tool for the McKinsey consultants in the problem-solving process are logic trees (which we discussed in Chapter 8), as "they make it easy to see the structure of the problem."[9]

Once they have a good overview of the factors that influence the problem, the consultants narrow the focus of their efforts. They primarily work on those issues that have the biggest impact on the problem and—very importantly—that they can actually influence (remember our I^2 matrix from Chapter 10).

Charles Conn uses an example from a consulting assignment that he completed for an environmental conservation foundation. The problem that he and his colleagues had to work on was how to save Pacific salmon. That's quite a big and complex problem!

"With salmon, ocean conditions turned out to be a big lever, but not one that we could adjust," Conn explains. He decided to focus the attention on fish habitats and fish-harvesting practices instead, as these were levers which he saw as both "big and movable."[10]

Once they found a solution for the "big and movable" issue, the consultants needed to convince the decision makers that their solution was actually the right thing to do. The tool that they used for this task is storytelling.

"Storytelling?" you might ask. "How can telling stories help to solve problems?"

Actually, this is a crucial part of the problem-solving process. As we discussed in Chapter 11, in many situations, you will only be able to solve the problem if you get the commitment of other people. Good stories are usually far more persuasive than dry facts. They create emotional resonance, and they can inspire and motivate people. "Until you motivate people to action," says Simon London, McKinsey's Global Director of Digital Communications, "you actually haven't solved anything."[11]

 What smart problem solvers can learn from consultants

Break your problem apart into more manageable issues and focus on the ones that are "big and movable."

Tell a compelling story to motivate others to help you solve the problem.

Solve it like an expert negotiator

Many problems arise because of a clash of interests between people. A common way to settle such differences is to conduct a negotiation. The main aim of a negotiation is to find a way to resolve an issue which is acceptable for all parties involved.

Among the world's most renowned experts on negotiation are Roger Fisher, William Ury and Bruce Patton from Harvard University. Together they wrote *Getting to Yes*, a perennial bestseller, and developed a negotiation strategy that helped millions of people achieve better outcomes both for their negotiation partners and themselves.[12] Their *principled negotiations* approach can help to overcome 'win-lose battles' in which each party just tries to get a bigger share of the cake to the detriment of their counterpart.

In these 'battles' (which are also called *positional bargaining*), the negotiators typically open the discussion with their respective positions. For example, one negotiator will say "The highest price that I would pay for this is 500 dollars," and the other one responds with "I will not sell for below 1,000 dollars." This is followed by a bargaining process until the negotiators eventually meet somewhere in between (maybe agreeing on 750 dollars in this particular case).

Positional bargaining tends to get us into an adversarial mindset. The negotiation becomes a zero-sum game, in which one party's gain is the other's loss.

Principled negotiations are different. They are not about winning, but about satisfying both parties' interests while at the same time taking care about preserving—and maybe even strengthening—the relationship between them.

So how do principled negotiations work?

There are four basic principles that Fisher, Ury and Patton propose a smart negotiator follows:

1. **Separate people from problems.** Smart negotiators refrain from blaming or attacking the other person (which in most cases just leads to a spiral of negative emotions). They will avoid entangling personal issues with the problem and treat each other as partners in the problem-solving process instead. They engage in a real dialogue,

which particularly means that they try to listen carefully and really understand the other party's interests and needs.

2. **Focus on interests (rather than on positions).** Let us take the following example: two people are fighting over the fishing rights to part of a river (let us assume that only one person can claim these rights). Both parties have a clear position: they want to get the rights. If—instead of entrenching themselves in their positions—the two parties started to explore their underlying interests first, they would maybe find a way to satisfy the interests of both sides. Maybe one of them has a big passion for fishing, while the other one is more interested in opening a fishing business. So they could actually form a team and found a fishing company that secures the fishing rights, with one person being responsible for fishing and the other for the commercial aspects of the business. The purpose of a principled negotiation is to serve the interests of the parties involved. Smart negotiators will therefore clearly explain their own interests and try to understand the interests of everyone else involved, too.

3. **Create options together.** When the underlying interests of all parties are well understood, it is time to find clever options together—options that will serve the interests of both sides. "Low cost for you and high benefit to them, and vice versa"[13]—that's the type of options that Fisher, Ury and Patton suggest us to look for in particular (Chapter 9 in this book has further ideas of how to generate more options for solving a problem in a mutually beneficial way).

4. **Use objective criteria.** With a range of different options on the table, smart negotiators will use objective criteria to choose the best solution. 'Objective' means that the criteria are independent of each side's interests. It is about finding a fair standard that can be used as a basis for an agreement. Examples of objective criteria include industry averages for a salary negotiation, local market prices for a real estate deal, cost estimates from experts, a legal precedent, professional standards, or traditions that are typically followed in a certain domain. Whatever the criteria, it is important that the negotiators agree on them in advance, so that the negotiation can be based on facts rather than on opinions.

With these four principles in mind—and with a shift in their negotiation goal from persuasion to joint problem solving—smart negotiators should be able to reach wise agreements with benefits for all sides.

What smart problem solvers can learn from expert negotiators

In problems that involve other people, listen carefully to understand their underlying interests, create options that satisfy the interests of all sides, and use objective criteria to choose the best solution.

Solve it like a coach

Good coaches—whether executive coaches or life coaches—use a smart questioning approach to help you think through challenging issues.[14] They listen and observe. Sometimes, they might also provide you with helpful feedback. But they do not solve problems for you.

Good coaches do not tell you what you should do. Instead, they use clever questions to stimulate your own critical and goal-oriented thinking about a problem. Thus, they actually help you solve your problem yourself.

One tool that many coaches around the world use is the GROW model (GROW stands for *Goal–Reality–Options–Will*). This is a framework for structuring a coaching conversation in four phases:[15]

- *Goal:* What do you want to achieve?
- *Reality:* What's the current situation?
- *Options:* Which options do you have to improve the situation?
- *Will:* What exactly will you do to make it happen?

Note that there are certain overlaps with our '5C' model of problem solving here. Knowing your goals is part of the 'Clarify' stage, investigating reality is part of the 'Causes' stage, and developing and choosing options are part of the 'Create' and 'Choose' stages—and then you hopefully will take action in the 'Commit' stage.

In each of the four phases of the GROW model, a coach will ask goal-oriented questions that help the person who is being coached better understand and make progress in their problem situation. Here are some examples of the types of question that a coach might ask.

COACHING QUESTIONS (EXAMPLES)[16]

Questions for the 'Goal' phase:

- *"What exactly would you like to have accomplished in three months/a year/...?"*
- *"What is your ultimate goal? What would things look like if you achieve it?"*
- *"What makes this goal so important for you?"*
- *"What are the main milestones on the way to achieving this goal? When would you need to reach them?"*
- *"How could you set a goal so it primarily depends on your actions and performance rather than on the circumstances or on what others do?"*
- *"How will you know that you have achieved your performance goal? How will you measure success?"*

Questions for the 'Reality' phase:

- *"What are the main factors that contributed to this situation?"*
- *"Who else is involved in this issue? What is their role?"*
- *"Which steps have you already taken to tackle this issue?"*
- *"What happened as a consequence?"*
- *"What are the main obstacles?"*
- *"What are your main concerns?"*
- *"What holds you back from taking action?"*

Questions for the 'Options' phase:

- *"What could be a potential solution here?"*
- *"What choices do you have?"*
- *"What advice would you give to someone else who is in the same situation as you are?"*
- *"What did you do when you were in a similar situation before?"*

- *"What could you do to remove this obstacle?"*
- *"How would you proceed if you had more money/time/information/...?"*
- *"Who could help you here? Who knows more about this? Who has done something like this before?"*
- *"Which of these options do you see as the most promising one (and why)?"*

Questions for the 'Will' phase:

- *"Which option will you pursue to achieve your goal?"*
- *"Which concrete action steps will you take?"*
- *"What will be your next step to make it happen?"*
- *"When (exactly) will you do this?"*
- *"Whose support do you need to make it happen? What exactly will you do (and when) to get that support?"*
- *"What are the main obstacles that you expect to see when you implement your actions?*
- *"How will you overcome these obstacles?"*
- *"On a scale of 1 to 10, how committed are you to taking this step?"*
- *"What would have to change to turn your commitment from 7 to 10?"*

If you do not have a coach yet (which might be useful to think about), try to ask yourself these questions. They might help you explore the problem that you are faced with in more depth.

By the way, the questions in the box above are taken from my book *Developing Coaching Skills: A Concise Introduction.* You are kindly invited to check it out if you are interested in how effective coaching works and how coaches help other people solve their problems. You will find more than 200 powerful coaching questions in the book.

What smart problem solvers can learn from coaches

Ask clever questions that stimulate critical and goal-oriented thinking during the problem-solving process.

Notes

Introduction

1. 5C models with similar wordings have also been proposed in other domains. One salient example is the 5C model ('Clarify', 'Conquer', 'Choose', 'Celebrate' and 'Commit') presented in the highly recommendable book *Change Your Life in 5: Practical Steps to Making Meaningful Changes in Your Life* by the award-winning London-based leadership and career coach Sue Belton (London: Welbeck Publishing 2020).
2. World Economic Forum (2020). *The Future of Jobs Report* (Cologny/Geneva: World Economic Forum).

Chapter 1: Problems are there to be solved

1. Mandela, N. (1994). Speech by Nelson Mandela announcing the ANC election victory. http://db.nelsonmandela.org/speeches/pub_view.asp?pg=item&ItemID=NMS174&txtstr=Carlton%20Hotel, accessed 4 March 2021.
2. Wright, W. (1900). Wilbur Wright to Octave Chanute, Dayton, May 13, 1900. https://invention.psychology.msstate.edu/i/Wrights/library/Chanute_Wright_correspond/May13-1900.html, accessed 4 April 2021.
3. Keller, H. (1903). *The Story of My Life*, Chapter IV. http://www.gutenberg.org/files/2397/2397-h/2397-h.htm, accessed 4 March 2021.
4. Keller, H. (1929). *Midstream: My Later Life* (New York, NY: Doubleday, Doran & Company), p. 214.
5. Voltaire (1918). Candide. https://www.gutenberg.org/files/19942/19942-h/19942-h.htm, accessed 16 February 2021.
6. Keller, H. (1903). *Optimism: An Essay* (New York, NY: T.Y. Crowell), p. 67.
7. Maxwell, J. (2018). *Developing the Leader Within You 2.0* (New York, NY: HarperCollins Leadership), p. 99.
8. Obama, B. (2008). Barack Obama's New Hampshire primary speech. https://www.nytimes.com/2008/01/08/us/politics/08text-obama.html, published 8 January 2008, accessed 16 February 2021.
9. Chang, E. C. (1998). Hope, problem-solving ability, and coping in a college student population: Some implications for theory and practice. *Journal of Clinical Psychology, 54*(7), 953–962.
10. Williams, G. (2014). Optimistic problem-solving activity: Enacting confidence, persistence, and perseverance. *ZDM Mathematics Education, 46*(3), 407–422.
11. Assad, K. K., Donnellan, M. B., & Conger, R. D. (2007). Optimism: An enduring resource for romantic relationships. *Journal of Personality and Social Psychology, 93*(2), 285–297.
12. Mayo Clinic (2021). Cognitive behavioral theory. https://www.mayoclinic.org/tests-procedures/cognitive-behavioral-therapy/about/pac-20384610, accessed 4 August 2021; Williams, H., & Palmer, S. (2018). CLARITY: A case study application of a cognitive behavioural coaching model. *European Journal of Applied Positive Psychology, 2*(6), 2397-7116.

Chapter 2: Believe in your abilities

1. Greene, B. (1991). When Jordan cried behind closed doors. https://www.chicagotribune.com/news/ct-xpm-1991-05-15-9102120922-story.html, published 15 May 1991, accessed 17 February 2021.

2. Stibel, J. (2017). Michael Jordan: A profile in failure. https://csq.com/2017/08/michael-jordan-profile-failure/#.YCzS6HkxIPY, published 29 August 2017, accessed 17 February 2017.
3. The concepts of growth mindset and fixed mindset are based on the work of Dweck, C. S. (2017). *Mindset: Changing the Way You Think to Fulfil Your Potential*, updated edition (London: Robinson).
4. Varol, O. (2020). *Think Like A Rocket Scientist: Simple Strategies You Can Use to Make Giant Leaps in Work and Life* (New York, NY: PublicAffairs), p. 232.
5. This story is based on Snow, S. (2014). *Smartcuts: How Hackers, Innovators, and Icons Accelerate Success* (New York, NY: HarperCollins); and Varol, O. (2020), op. cit.
6. Varol, O. (2020), op. cit., p. 231.
7. Snow, S. (2014), op. cit.
8. Dweck, C. S., & Yeager, D. S. (2019). Mindsets: A view from two eras. *Perspectives on Psychological Science, 14*(3), 481–496; Yeager, D. S., Hanselman, P., Walton, G. M., Murray, J. S., Crosnoe, R., Muller, C., & Dweck, C. S. (2019). A national experiment reveals where a growth mindset improves achievement. *Nature, 573*(7774), 364–369.
9. Atitumpong, A., & Badir, Y. F. (2018). Leader-member exchange, learning orientation and innovative work behavior. *Journal of Workplace Learning, 30*(1), 32–47.
10. Mutonyi, B. R., Slåtten, T., & Lien, G. (2020). Empowering leadership, work group cohesiveness, individual learning orientation and individual innovative behaviour in the public sector: Empirical evidence from Norway. *International Journal of Public Leadership, 16*(2), 175–197.
11. A similar process was proposed by Belostikova, P. (2020). Fixed and growth mindset: How to switch from "I can't do it" to "I can do it." https://leaderdecision.com/fixed-and-growth-mindset-how-to-switch-from-i-cant-do-it-to-i-can-do-it/, published 13 April 2020, accessed 4 October 2021.

Chapter 3: Focus on what you can influence

1. For a more detailed account of the life of Marcus Aurelius see Holiday, R., & Hanselman, S. (2020). *Lives of the Stoics: The Art of Living from Zeno to Marcus Aurelius* (New York, NY: Portfolio/Penguin), pp. 278–299.
2. Epictetus (1890). *The Works of Epictetus: His Discourses, in Four Books, the Enchiridion, and Fragments*. Translated by Thomas Wentworth Higginson (New York, NY: Thomas Nelson and Sons).
3. Marcus Aurelius (2017). *The Meditations of the Emperor Marcus Aurelius Antoninus: A New Rendering Based on the Foulis Translation of 1742*, Book IV (32). http://www.gutenberg.org/files/55317/55317-h/55317-h.htm, published 9 August 2017, accessed 5 April 2021. Slightly adapted into more modern English by the author.
4. Marcus Aurelius (1944). *The Meditations of the Emperor Marcus Antoninus*. Translated by Arthur Spenser Loat Farquharson (London: Oxford University Press), Book VIII (32).
5. ibid., Book VIII (50).
6. ibid., Book VIII (47).
7. Roberts D. (2020). Michael Phelps to Tokyo Olympics 2021 athletes: 'Focus on what you can control'. https://ca.finance.yahoo.com/news/michael-phelps-to-tokyo-olympics-2021-athletes-focus-on-what-you-can-control-193907959.html, published 9 December 2020, accessed 18 February 2021.
8. Bhargava, S., & Pradhan, H. (2018). Effect of goal orientation on job performance: Moderating effect of situational strength at work. *Journal of Management Research, 18*(2), 90–101.
9. Gardner, E. A. (2006). Instruction in mastery goal orientation: Developing problem solving and persistence for clinical settings. *Journal of Nursing Education, 45*(9), 343–347.

Chapter 4: Use the power of your unconscious mind

1. Klarreich, E. (2013). Unheralded mathematician bridges the prime gap. https://www. quantamagazine.org/yitang-zhang-proves-landmark-theorem-in-distribution-of-prime-numbers-20130519/, published 19 May 2013, accessed 19 February 2021.
2. ibid.
3. The whole story is based on the account of Klarreich (2013), op. cit.; the story was also retold in a similar way by Nisbett, R. (2016). *Mindware: Tools for Smart Thinking* (London: Penguin Books).
4. Varol (2020) reported on the stories of Einstein, Heisenberg, and Rowling (Varol, O. (2020). *Think Like A Rocket Scientist: Simple Strategies You Can Use to Make Giant Leaps in Work and Life* (New York, NY: PublicAffairs)).
5. Nisbett, R. (2016), op. cit, p. 66.
6. Nisbett, R. (2016), op. cit.
7. Varol, O. (2020), op. cit., pp. 90–91.
8. Gilhooly, K. J., Georgiou, G., & Devery, U. (2013). Incubation and creativity: Do something different. *Thinking & Reasoning, 19*(2), 137–149.
9. Tan, T., Zou, H., Chen, C., & Luo, J. (2015). Mind wandering and the incubation effect in insight problem solving. *Creativity Research Journal, 27*(4), 375–382.
10. Gable, S. L., Hopper, E. A., & Schooler, J. W. (2019). When the muses strike: Creative ideas of physicists and writers routinely occur during mind wandering. *Psychological Science, 30*(3), 396–404.

Chapter 5: Rally your support team

1. This question was also suggested by Maxwell, J. (2018). *Developing the Leader Within You 2.0* (New York, NY: HarperCollins Leadership), p. 108.
2. Wedell-Wedellsborg, T. (2020). *What's Your Problem? To Solve Your Toughest Problems, Change the Problems You Solve* (Boston, MA: Harvard Business Review Press), p. 31.
3. ibid., p. 131.
4. Lash, J. P. (1980). *Helen and Teacher: The Story of Helen Keller and Anne Sullivan Macy* (New York, NY: Delacorte Press/Seymour Lawrence), p. 489.
5. Jordan, M. (1994). *I Can't Accept Not Trying: Michael Jordan on the Pursuit of Excellence* (San Francisco, CA: HarperSanFrancisco), pp. 20–24.
6. Laughlin, P. R., Hatch, E. C., Silver, J. S., & Boh, L. (2006). Groups perform better than the best individuals on letters-to-numbers problems: Effects of group size. *Journal of Personality and Social Psychology, 90*(4), 644–651.
7. Maciejovsky, B., Sutter, M., Budescu, D. V., & Bernau, P. (2013). Teams make you smarter: How exposure to teams improves individual decisions in probability and reasoning tasks. *Management Science, 59*(6), 1255–1270.
8. Hargadon, A. B., & Bechky, B. A. (2006). When collections of creatives become creative collectives: A field study of problem solving at work. *Organization Science, 17*(4), 484–500.

Chapter 6: Beware of common problem-solving errors

1. This story is based on Bregman, P. (2015). Are you trying to solve the wrong problem? https://hbr.org/2015/12/are-you-solving-the-wrong-problem, published 7 December 2015, accessed 4 March 2021.
2. Griffiths, C., & Costi, M. (2019). *The Creative Thinking Handbook: Your Step-by-Step Guide to Problem Solving in Business* (London: Kogan Page).
3. Varol, O. (2020). *Think Like A Rocket Scientist: Simple Strategies You Can Use to Make Giant Leaps in Work and Life* (New York, NY: PublicAffairs), p. 62.
4. ibid., p. 51.
5. Nisbett, R. (2016). *Mindware: Tools for Smart Thinking* (London: Penguin Books), p. 39.
6. ibid.
7. Reiter-Palmon, R., Mumford, M. D., & Threlfall, K. V. (1998). Solving everyday problems creatively: The role of problem construction and personality type. *Creativity Research Journal, 11*(3), 187–197.
8. Abdulla, A. M., Paek, S. H., Cramond, B., & Runco, M. A. (2020). Problem finding and creativity: A meta-analytic review. *Psychology of Aesthetics, Creativity, and the Arts, 14*(1), 3–14.
9. Mendel, R., Traut-Mattausch, E., Jonas, E., Leucht, S., Kane, J. M., Maino, K., Kissling, W., & Hamann, J. (2011). Confirmation bias: Why psychiatrists stick to wrong preliminary diagnoses. *Psychological Medicine, 41*(12), 2651–2659.
10. Nisbett, R. (2016), op. cit., p. 117.

Chapter 7: Clarify—Solve the right problem

1. Einstein, A., & Infeld, L. (1971). *The Evolution of Physics: The Growth of Ideas from Early Concepts to Relativity and Quanta.* 2nd ed., re-issued (Cambridge: Cambridge University Press), p. 92.
2. Bhardwaj, G., Crocker, A., Sims, J., & Wang, R. D. (2018). Alleviating the plunging-in bias, elevating strategic problem-solving. *Academy of Management Learning & Education, 17*(3), 279–301.
3. Wedell-Wedellsborg, T. (2020). *What's Your Problem? To Solve Your Toughest Problems, Change the Problems You Solve* (Boston, MA: Harvard Business Review Press), p. 41.
4. Griffiths, C., & Costi, M. (2019). *The Creative Thinking Handbook: Your Step-by-Step Guide to Problem Solving in Business* (London: Kogan Page).
5. Rasiel, E. M. & Friga, P. N. (2002). *The McKinsey Mind* (New York, NY: McGraw-Hill), p. 17.
6. Repenning, N. P., Kieffer, D., & Astor, T. (2017). The most underrated skill in management. *MIT Sloan Management Review, 58*(3), 39–48, p. 39.
7. ibid., pp. 41–42.
8. Schwartz, B. (2016). *The Paradox of Choice: Why More Is Less.* Revised and updated edition (New York, NY: HarperCollins), p. 88.
9. Wedell-Wedellsborg, T. (2020). op. cit., p. 5.
10. ibid., p. 20.
11. Wedell-Wedellsborg (2020), op. cit.
12. ibid. (2020), p. 29.
13. Repenning et al. (2017), op. cit., pp. 41–42.
14. Getzels, J. W., & Csikszentmihalyi, M. (1976). *The Creative Vision: A Longitudinal Study of Problem Finding in Art* (New York, NY: John Wiley & Sons).

15. van Hooijdonk, M., Mainhard, T., Kroesbergen, E. H., & van Tartwijk, J. (2020). Creative problem solving in primary education: Exploring the role of fact finding, problem finding, and solution finding across tasks. *Thinking Skills and Creativity, 37*, https://doi. org/10.1016/j.tsc.2020.100665.
16. Runco, M. A., & Okuda, S. M. (1988). Problem discovery, divergent thinking, and the creative process. *Journal of Youth and Adolescence, 17*(3), 211–220.
17. Nutt, P. C. (1999). Surprising but true: Half the decisions in organizations fail. *Academy of Management Perspectives, 13*(4), 75–90, pp. 75; 80.

Chapter 8: Causes—Make the right diagnosis

1. This story—including the direct quotes—is based on rtl.de (2018). Falsche Medikation bei Pfeifferschem Drüsenfieber: Wegen eines Antibiotikums wäre Celina (12) fast erstickt. https://www.rtl.de/cms/falsche-medikation-bei-pfeifferschem-druesenfieber-we-gen-eines-antibiotikums-waere-celina-12-fast-erstickt-4119044.html, published 14 March 2018, accessed 11 March 2021.
2. Doyle, A. C. (1892). *The Adventures of Sherlock Holmes* (New York, NY: Harper & Brothers), p. 7.
3. Wanatabe, K. (2009). *Problem Solving 101: A Simple Book for Smart People* (London: Vermilion), S. 26.
4. Doyle (1892), op. cit., p. 289.
5. Doyle, A. C. (1893). *The Adventures of Sherlock Holmes*. 2nd ed. (London: George Newnes), p. 83.
6. The 'Zany Ones' quote and the whole story is based on a Wikipedia article about the reliability of Wikipedia, https://en.wikipedia.org/wiki/Reliability_of_Wikipedia#Nota-ble_incidents, accessed 12 March 2021—and please note that I cannot guarantee this information is 100 percent reliable.
7. Doyle, A. C. (1894). *Memoirs of Sherlock Holmes* (New York, NY: A. L. Burt Company), p. 22.
8. Rasiel, E. M. & Friga, P. N. (2002). *The McKinsey Mind* (New York, NY: McGraw-Hill).
9. Doyle (1892), op. cit., p. 281.
10. Varol, O. (2020). *Think Like A Rocket Scientist: Simple Strategies You Can Use to Make Giant Leaps in Work and Life* (New York, NY: PublicAffairs), p. 173.
11. ibid., p. 173.
12. Please note that the author does not have a medical education. The author and publisher cannot give any guarantee for the medical information that is included in this chapter. All the descriptions here are merely made for the purpose of illustrating a problem-solving process.
13. Doyle, A. C. (1902). *The Hound of the Baskervilles* (New York, NY: Grosset & Dunlap), p. 4.
14. Schiff, G. D., Hasan, O., Kim, S., Abrams, R., Cosby, K., et al. (2009). Diagnostic error in medicine: Analysis of 583 physician-reported errors. *Archives of Internal Medicine, 169*(20), 1881–1887.
15. Kim, S., Alison, L., & Christiansen, P. (2020). The impact of individual differences on investigative hypothesis generation under time pressure. *International Journal of Police Science & Management, 22*(2), 171–182.
16. Müller, R., Gögel, C., & Bönsel, R. (2020). Data or interpretations: Impacts of information presentation strategies on diagnostic processes. *Human Factors and Ergonomics in Manufacturing & Service Industries, 30*(4), 266–281.
17. Mesmer-Magnus, J. R., & DeChurch, L. A. (2009). Information sharing and team performance: A meta-analysis. *Journal of Applied Psychology, 94*(2), 535–546.

Chapter 9: Create—Find promising solutions

1. Head, W. D. (1935). Home-town international service: An 'adventure in friendship'. *The Rotarian, 47*(4), 38–43.
2. This story is based on the account of Mahatma Gandhi's grandson Arun Gandhi (Gandhi, A. (2017). *The Gift of Anger* (London: Penguin Michael Joseph), pp. 37–40).
3. Catchpole, K. R., De Leval, M. R., McEwan, A., Pigott, N., Elliott, M. J., McQuillan, A., MacDonald, C., & Goldman, A. J. (2007). Patient handover from surgery to intensive care: using Formula 1 pit-stop and aviation models to improve safety and quality. *Pediatric Anesthesia, 17*(5), 470–478.
4. Wedell-Wedellsborg, T. (2020). *What's Your Problem? To Solve Your Toughest Problems, Change the Problems You Solve* (Boston, MA: Harvard Business Review Press).
5. Rasiel, E. M. & Friga, P. N. (2002). *The McKinsey Mind* (New York, NY: McGraw-Hill), p. 62.
6. Osborn, A. F. (1953). *Applied Imagination* (York, NY: Charles Scribner's Sons).
7. Furnham, A. (2000). The brainstorming myth. *Business Strategy Review, 11*(4), 21–28.
8. Griffiths, C., & Costi, M. (2019). *The Creative Thinking Handbook: Your Step-by-Step Guide to Problem Solving in Business* (London: Kogan Page).
9. ibid. (2019).
10. Bodell, L. (2016). *Kill the Company: End the Status Quo, Start an Innovation Revolution* (London: Routledge).
11. Wanatabe, K. (2009). *Problem Solving 101: A Simple Book for Smart People* (London: Vermilion).
12. Waldrop, M. (2017). Einstein's relativity explained in 4 simple steps. https://www.nationalgeographic.com/science/article/einstein-relativity-thought-experiment-train-lightning-genius, published 16 May 2017, accessed 16 March 2021.
13. Einstein A. (1954). On the method of theoretical physics. In: Einstein, A., *Ideas and Opinions,* pp. 270–276 (New York, NY: Crown Publishing).
14. Griffiths & Costi (2019), op. cit.
15. Wedell-Wedellsborg, T. (2020), op. cit.
16. Scotney, V. S., Weissmeyer, S., Carbert, N., & Gabora, L. (2019). The ubiquity of cross-domain thinking in the early phase of the creative process. *Frontiers in Psychology, 10*, https://doi.org/10.3389/fpsyg.2019.01426
17. Montag-Smit, T., & Maertz Jr, C. P. (2017). Searching outside the box in creative problem solving: The role of creative thinking skills and domain knowledge. *Journal of Business Research, 81* (December), 1–10.
18. Ward, T. B., Patterson, M. J., & Sifonis, C. M. (2004). The role of specificity and abstraction in creative idea generation. *Creativity Research Journal, 16*(1), 1–9.
19. Paulus, P. B., & Yang, H. C. (2000). Idea generation in groups: A basis for creativity in organizations. *Organizational Behavior and Human Decision Processes, 82*(1), 76–87.
20. Girotra, K., Terwiesch, C., & Ulrich, K. T. (2010). Idea generation and the quality of the best idea. *Management Science, 56*(4), 591–605.
21. Puccio, G. J., Burnett, C., Acar, S., Yudess, J. A., Holinger, M., & Cabra, J. F. (2020). Creative problem solving in small groups: The effects of creativity training on idea generation, solution creativity, and leadership effectiveness. *The Journal of Creative Behavior, 54*(2), 453–471.

Chapter 10: Choose—Decide on the optimal solution

1. Clapham, W. (2013). Positive tickets: A new way to police. https://www.theguardian.com/commentisfree/2013/feb/20/positive-tickets-police-alternative, published 20 February 2013, accessed 18 March 2021.
2. ibid.
3. ibid.
4. Sprenger, R. K. (2020). In der Coronakrise konnte man nicht falsch entscheiden. https://www.kleinezeitung.at/international/corona/5831243/Essay_In-der-Coronakrise-konnte-man-nicht-falsch-entscheiden, published 26 June 2020, accessed 18 March 2021.
5. Griffiths, C., & Costi, M. (2019). *The Creative Thinking Handbook: Your Step-by-Step Guide to Problem Solving in Business* (London: Kogan Page); Wanatabe, K. (2009). *Problem Solving 101: A Simple Book for Smart People* (London: Vermilion).
6. Griffiths & Costi (2019), op. cit.
7. Wanatabe (2009).
8. Nisbett, R. (2016). *Mindware: Tools for Smart Thinking* (London: Penguin Books), p. 86.
9. Bell, D. E. (1982). Regret in decision making under uncertainty. *Operations Research, 30*(5), 961–981; Sternad, D. (2020). *Effective Management: Developing Yourself, Others and Organizations* (London: Red Globe Press/Macmillan International Higher Education).
10. Ware, B. (2019). *Top Five Regrets of the Dying: A Life Transformed by the Dearly Departing* (Alexandria, NSW: Hay House Australia).
11. Similar questions were proposed by the British psychotherapist and recovery coach Beth Burgess (Burgess, B. (no date). 7 questions you should ask yourself when faced with a tough decision in life. https://www.lifehack.org/articles/communication/7-questions-you-should-ask-yourself-when-faced-with-tough-decision-life.html, accessed 18 March 2021). Burgess also suggests two additional questions which are both similar to the 'no regrets' check.
12. Ware, B. (2019), op. cit.
13. Clapham, W. (2012). Listening and acting are two ends of the same stick. blog.ward-clapham.com/listening-and-acting-are-two-ends-of-the-same-stick, published 25 March 2012, accessed 20 March 2021.
14. Dar-Nimrod, I., Rawn, C. D., Lehman, D. R., & Schwartz, B. (2009). The maximization paradox: The costs of seeking alternatives. *Personality and Individual Differences, 46*(5–6), 631–635.
15. Schwartz, B., Ward, A., Monterosso, J., Lyubomirsky, S., White, K., & Lehman, D. R. (2002). Maximizing versus satisficing: Happiness is a matter of choice. *Journal of Personality and Social Psychology, 83*(5), 1178–1197.
16. Sweis, B. M., Abram, S. V., Schmidt, B. J., Seeland, K. D., MacDonald, A. W., Thomas, M. J., & Redish, A. D. (2018). Sensitivity to "sunk costs" in mice, rats, and humans. *Science, 361*(6398), 178–181.
17. Brewer, N. T., DeFrank, J. T., & Gilkey, M. B. (2016). Anticipated regret and health behavior: A meta-analysis. *Health Psychology, 35*(11), 1264–1275.
18. Bjälkebring, P., Västfjäll, D., Svenson, O., & Slovic, P. (2016). Regulation of experienced and anticipated regret in daily decision making. *Emotion, 16*(3), 381–386.

Chapter 11: Commit—Make it happen

1. The Dyson story as reported here is based on James Dyson's own account in Helm, B. (2012). How I did it: James Dyson. https://www.inc.com/magazine/201203/burt-helm/how-i-did-it-james-dyson.html, published 28 February 2012, accessed 21 March 2021
2. ibid.
3. Goodman, N. (2012). James Dyson on using failure to drive success. https://www.entrepreneur.com/article/224855, published 5 November 2012, accessed 21 March 2021.
4. During the editing process of this book, I noticed that the Plan–Test–Review–Learn loop closely resembles the PDCA cycle (Plan–Do–Check–Act), a management method that is used in continuous improvement initiatives. The PDCA cycle is used in countless organizations to solve operational problems and improve production and service processes.
5. Goodman (2012), op. cit.
6. Varol, O. (2020). *Think Like A Rocket Scientist: Simple Strategies You Can Use to Make Giant Leaps in Work and Life* (New York, NY: PublicAffairs), p. 193.
7. Curtin, M. (2017). Billionaire CEO Sara Blakely says these 7 words are the best career advice she ever got. https://www.inc.com/melanie-curtin/billionaire-ceo-sara-blakely-says-these-7-words-are-best-career-advice-she-ever-got.html, published 29 September 2017, accessed 23 March 2021.
8. Fortune (2012). The best advice I ever got. https://fortune.com/2012/10/25/the-best-advice-i-ever-got/, published 25 October 2012, accessed 23 March 2021.
9. This quote was attributed to Margaret Mead by various authors, e.g. by Lutkehaus, N. C. (2008). *Margaret Mead: The Making of an American Icon* (Princeton, NJ: Princeton University Press), p. 4, although no-one really knows the original source.
10. Maxwell, J. (2018). *Developing the Leader Within You 2.0* (New York, NY: HarperCollins Leadership), p. 109.
11. Radcliffe, S. (2012). *Leadership Plain and Simple* (Harlow: Pearson Education), p. 59.
12. Goodman, N. (2012), op. cit.
13. Lucas, B. J., & Nordgren, L. F. (2015). People underestimate the value of persistence for creative performance. *Journal of Personality and Social Psychology, 109*(2), 232–243.
14. Ericsson, K. A. (2004). Deliberate practice and the acquisition and maintenance of expert performance in medicine and related domains. *Academic Medicine, 79*(10), S70–S81; Ericsson, K. A. (2015). Acquisition and maintenance of medical expertise: A perspective from the expert-performance approach with deliberate practice. *Academic Medicine, 90*(11), 1471–1486.
15. Ericsson, K. A. (2006). The influence of experience and deliberate practice on the development of superior expert performance. In Ericsson, K. A., Charness, N., Feltovich, P. J., & Hoffmann, R. R. (eds.), *The Cambridge Handbook of Expertise and Expert Performance*, pp. 683–704 (Cambridge: Cambridge University Press).
16. Bachkirova, T., Arthur, L., & Reading, E. (2021). Evaluating a coaching and mentoring program: Challenges and solutions. In: Passmore, J., & Tee, D. (eds), *Coaching Researched: A Coaching Psychology Reader*, pp. 361–378 (Hoboken, NJ: Wiley); Sternad, D. (2021). *Developing Coaching Skills: A Concise Introduction* (Moosburg: econcise).

Conclusion: Problem solved!

1. Lao-Tze (1919). *Laotzu's Tao and Wu Wei* (New York, NY: Brentano's), p. 44.

Appendix: Solve it like the pros

1. Hawking, S. (1988). *A Brief History of Time* (New York, NY: Bantam Books), p. 10.
2. The general diagnosis process in healthcare as it is described here and in the following is based on Balogh, E. P., Miller, B. T., & Ball, J. R. (2015). *Improving Diagnosis in Health Care* (Washington, DC: The National Academies Press).
3. ibid., p. 36.
4. Hasso Plattner Institute of Design (no date). An introduction to design thinking: Process guide. https://web.stanford.edu/~mshanks/MichaelShanks/files/509554.pdf, accessed 24 March 2021
5. ibid.
6. forbes.com (no date). McKinsey & Company. https://www.forbes.com/companies/mckinsey-company/, accessed 25 March 2021.
7. McLean, R. & Conn, C. (2018). *Bulletproof Problem Solving* (Hoboken, NJ: John Wiley & Sons), pp. xviii–xix.
8. London, S., Sarrazin, H., & Conn, C. (2019). How to master the seven-steps problem-solving process. https://www.mckinsey.com/business-functions/strategy-and-corporate-finance/our-insights/how-to-master-the-seven-step-problem-solving-process, published 13 September 2019, accessed 25 March 2021.
9. McLean & Conn (2018), op. cit., p. 20.
10. London et al. (2019), op. cit.
11. ibid.
12. The ideas in the "Solve it like an expert negotiator" section are based on Fisher, R., Ury, W. L., & Patton, B. (1991). *Getting to Yes: Negotiating Agreement Without Giving In* (Boston/New York: Houghton Mifflin Company).
13. ibid., p. 76.
14. Sternad, D. (2021). *Developing Coaching Skills: A Concise Introduction* (Moosburg: econcise).
15. Whitmore, Sir J. (2017). *Coaching for Performance: The Principles and Practice of Coaching and Leadership*. 5th ed. (London/Boston: Nicholas Brealey Publishing).
16. The questions are taken from Sternad, D. (2021), op. cit.

Index

Dr Dietmar Sternad is Professor of International Management at CUAS (Carinthia University of Applied Sciences) with a passion for teaching his students how to become smart problem solvers. He won several national and international awards for teaching excellence and for the development of outstanding learning materials. Dietmar also has years of experience as an executive in book publishing and media companies, in strategy and leadership consulting, and in training and coaching top managers and high potentials. He is author of several internationally acclaimed textbooks, such as *Effective Management: Developing Yourself, Others and Organizations* (Macmillan International Higher Education) or the international bestseller *Developing Coaching Skills: A Concise Introduction* (econcise publishing). Dietmar has faced a lot of problems (and been able to solve quite a few) in his various roles as a media executive, researcher, entrepreneur, management consultant, and father of two children.

Learn how to coach effectively—
and help others unlock their potential!

- A compact yet comprehensive overview of **how coaching works**
- Over **200 powerful coaching questions** that you can apply right away
- Conduct effective **solution-oriented coaching conversations**
- **Best-practice insights** from experienced coaches
- **Practical coaching exercises** for developing your own coaching skills

Developing Coaching Skills: A Concise Introduction
is available wherever good books and ebooks are sold.

46481926R00090